# Zip

## Y O U R

# Lips

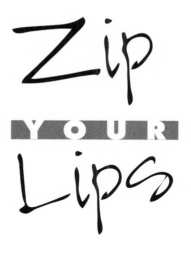

# Zip YOUR Lips

*A Parent's Guide to*
## BRIEF AND EFFECTIVE COMMUNICATION

### Dale M. Jacobs, M.D. &
### Renee Gordon Jacobs, M.S.W.

*Illustrations by*
### Ann Haaland

E L E M E N T

Boston, Massachusetts • Shaftesbury, Dorset
Melbourne, Victoria

Published in the USA in 1999 by
Element Books, Inc.
160 North Washington Street
Boston, MA 02114

Published in Great Britain in 1999 by
Element Books Limited
Shaftesbury, Dorset SP7 8BP

Published in Australia in 1999 by
Element Books Limited for
Penguin Australia Limited
487 Maroondah Highway, Ringwood, Victoria 3134

Library of Congress Cataloging-in-Publication Data

Jacobs, Dale M.
    Zip your lips : a parent's guide to brief and effective communication /
Dale M. Jacobs & Renee Gordon Jacobs ; illustrations by Ann Haaland.
        p.   cm.
    Includes bibliographical references and index.
    ISBN 1-86204-401-5 (pbk. : alk. paper)
      1. Parent and child.  2. Communication in the family.  3. Parenting.
      I. Title.
HQ755.85.J33 1999
649'.1 —dc21                              99-019529
                                          CIP

Printed and bound in the United States by Edwards Brothers

# Contents

## Illustrations

*This book is dedicated to*
*Rebecca, Joshua and Sarah—*
friends, teachers and delightful partners
in our parenting journey

# Acknowledgments

WE HAVE many people to thank for their important roles in our lives and in the development of this book.

Our parents were far from perfect, but they loved us very much and did the best they could. They would be so proud of the wonderful extended family that they began.

We have shared hopes, fears and struggles with so many families over the years. We honor them and thank them for all we learned, both from their successes and from their problems.

Some of our first supervisors when we began our training as psychotherapists were a source of guidance and inspiration. Much appreciation to Dr. Sara Dubo and Dr. Ralph Rabinowitch, founders and directors of Hawthorne Center in Northville, Michigan, and to Dr. Michael Green, director of the Child Guidance Clinic of Springfield, Massachusetts.

We have studied with and been influenced by some of the greatest therapists, including Salvador Minuchin, M.D., Jay Haley, Ph.D. and Rae Wiener, M.S.W., formerly at the Philadelphia Child Guidance Clinic; Virginia Satir and Jane

Parsons Fein, two very special women and teachers; Milton Erickson, M.D. and Harriet Hollander, Ph.D. Families have benefited so much from the inspired work and caring of these remarkable people.

Amy Zerner and Monte Farber, gifted artists, spiritual beings and dear friends, have influenced our lives in so many ways. Their inspiration enabled this book to become a reality.

Lori Solensten and Anne Marie Tague spent a great deal of time poring over the manuscripts. Their comments greatly enriched this work. Julie Sullivan was extremely helpful in her thorough editing. Finally, we would also like to thank Roberta Scimone for believing in *Zip Your Lips* and helping us get the word out to more parents.

# Introduction

HOW MANY times have we started to tell our children something—how to behave, how to do something the "right" way—only to have them roll their eyes, sigh and groan, or worse, give us the blank stare that means "I'm not listening"? This may be the most frequent parent-child scenario in every household. The reason? Parents talk too much!

We want so earnestly to give our children the benefit of our years of living and our painful mistakes. When they do not respond, we talk louder or use more words and repeat ourselves ad nauseam until we have woven a web of phrases so tightly around their little heads that we will never get through. We do need to instruct and guide them. But how do we get them to listen? How can we be effective communicators? The answer is simple: Be brief. Be direct. Be positive. Make every word count. Say the message in a way that invites the little darling or jaded teenager to listen and consider.

*Zip Your Lips* is a guide toward brief, more effective parent talk. It will save years of strain on our vocal cords. Eliminating all those unnecessary words gives us more time to enjoy being with our children. This is the secret: The less we talk, the more our children share with us and *the more willing they are to listen!* If this sounds just like the information you need, join us on this course in effective parent-child dialogue. We will be brief. We promise.

If we go back twenty or thirty years, it seems to us that there was less talking and more crisp messages like, "Just do it," "I'm the parent" and "Because I said so." Parents were quick to get the wooden spoon, to swat the behind. During a 1978 parenting workshop when the discussion turned to the difficulties of shopping with children, one quiet young mother told the others how she got her children to behave. She described how she would grab her daughter's shirt at the neck and tell her, "If you don't behave, I'm going to break your arm." We knew she wouldn't hurt a flea, but obviously her daughter had enough doubt to settle down and behave while Mom finished her errands.

In the seventies, the pendulum started swinging away from an authoritarian parenting style. Instead, parents were encouraged to explain and talk with their children, to run their household as a democracy, not a dictatorship. With the increase in reported incidences of child abuse, parents today are afraid to even mention physical punishment. Young children threaten to call the police if a parent or teacher touches them in a punitive way. Now parents are mostly talk, little action. It is painful in a store or restaurant to hear a parent saying fifty times, "If you don't behave, we are going to leave." The empty threat is repeated over and over, each time in a louder, more hostile tone. The child continues to misbehave, totally ignoring the parent's request, and the dance continues.

As part of a research study on parenting techniques, video cameras were placed in every room of one family's home. The camera recorded the mother yelling at her child to pick up her shoes. She repeated the request thirteen times while the child lay sprawled on the sofa watching television. Finally the mother picked up the shoes herself and put them in a closet. During a follow-up interview, the daughter laughingly explained that she never listens to mom because there are no consequences. *Zip Your Lips* will suggest ways to speak softly and effectively. In other words, to say less, say it quietly and firmly and get results much of the time. The book also emphasizes the power of positive messages—compliments, appreciation, loving words—as the most important tool to strengthen the parent-child relationship.

A note of caution: There are no magic formulas for raising children. Nothing works all the time, and the same approach may not work on different children. The ideas in this book are psychologically sound. They are meant as a guideline for parenting. It's important not to get discouraged if we try some of these techniques and do not get the desired results right away. It takes time to show our children that we are serious about this new approach. They are comfortable, most likely in an uncomfortable way, with our lectures and yelling. They know how to push the right buttons in an argument. They are adept at tuning us out or negotiating us down.

Hang in there. Once you make a commitment to this new language of "positive, brief talk," stay with it. Give it a chance to work. Too often parents will hear about a new technique and rush to try it. When it fails to produce immediate results, they give up and revert to the familiar ways. Children test us to see if we are serious, to see if we can endure their testing. It is healthy and helpful for them to test. It is equally helpful for us to hold firm.

Raising children cannot follow a precise equation, but child-rearing can be based on a combination of a guiding philosophy, acquired wisdom and intuition. Consider the ideas in this book as a recipe. Like any new cook, the first time you try a recipe you probably follow the directions explicitly. The second time you may adjust it or improvise a little. As you gain confidence and familiarity, you will stop measuring and add your own flair so it becomes something similar to but different from the original. Feel free to adjust and improvise to make these suggestions work for you and your family.

It is crucial to be patient with ourselves. We all do the best we can in this most difficult job. There is no such thing as a perfect parent! We all "lose it" at times; we all yell at times. When I was a young and very insecure mother, there were very few books on raising children. One author in the 1970s became well known for his writings on talking with children. Reading his suggested scripts, I and many other parents felt intimidated and upset with ourselves. We were not talking with our children in such calm, measured ways. It was comforting to learn that, in his own home with his own children, he yelled periodically.

On the other hand, I unwittingly intimidated other parents. When our own children were younger, clients would often say to me (Renee), "But you never yell at your children. You are so quiet and soft-spoken." I explained that of course I yelled at my children when I was at home. At work, in my office, where I did not have to run from one place to another and cope with three children, I was very calm and quiet. Our goal is not to be the perfect parent with the "right" response at all times, but to continue learning and improving our skills so we have the best chance to help our children to be loving, responsible and confident (not perfect) adults.

*Note:* The situations used as examples of parent-child interactions are composites drawn from our own and others' experiences. The names were selected randomly and do not represent any actual people. The concepts are generally applicable to situations with children of all ages. Where appropriate, examples will be given by the following age groups: preschooler, kindergarten through sixth grade, teenager and older. In addition to these categories, it is important to gear your response to your particular child's maturity level, temperament and learning style. Some children with Attention Deficit Disorder or learning disabilities are socially much younger than their chronological age. Some children are more mature. Gifted children may seem very mature because they are verbally quite articulate, but emotionally they may be age-level or below.

The examples are to be read as suggestions of positive, brief communication. The dialogues are not meant to imply that there is only one right way to say something to your children. Rather, they are the starting point for each of you to develop your own positive talk, using the examples as guidelines.

# 1

## Brevity Works Best

PARENTS with children who have Attention Deficit Disorder (ADD) or processing problems learn to give their children short, concise messages. If they want their child to get ready for bed, for example, they need to say, "Go get into your pajamas." Later they can give the next request, "Please wash your face and brush your teeth." If they make too general a statement, or request several things in the same breath, the child loses the message. To some extent, all children have a deficit disorder because they generally hear only what they want to hear and conveniently forget the rest.

For some reason that has nothing to do with intelligence, it seems to take the rest of us about twenty years of parenting (if we're lucky) to learn that our children do not hang on every word we say. In our desperation to get them to listen—and respond—we tend to ramble on in a whiny, demanding voice. This can be accompanied by name-calling or, even worse, obscenities. Bingo, we have lost them! Our pontifications have other results:

- *Our children get angry and plot to foil our efforts.*
- *They think we are idiotic and not worthy of their time.*
- *They learn that if they just wait us out, we will either do the job ourselves or forget what we asked.*
- *All of the above.*

Much of what we want to say to our children really is important and necessary to their development and to keeping our home running smoothly. It is imperative that we find ways to convey our messages so our children will listen and respect what we have to say.

The most important step is to keep all statements and requests brief. One or two sentences is best. This may be extremely hard to do at first. But try it for a while—the positive results will encourage you to continue this new way of speaking. Think about what you want to express. Then say it simply and directly, without a lot of explanation or embellishment.

For example, in the morning you might say, "We'll be leaving for school in ten minutes." It is not necessary to say, "We're leaving in ten minutes, and if you aren't ready, I'm leaving you home. You know I have to get to work and you always make me late. I'm sick of this fighting every morning." Your child knows you have to get to work, and she or he is probably sick of all the yelling, too. Your complaint serves no purpose other than to create more anger and tension.

When our child has done something wrong, we are most likely tempted to carry on in a loud voice. Too often we are led by the emotion of the moment into a humiliating (to the child) diatribe on other awful things she or he has done. It is much more effective to calm yourself first. Take a few deep breaths. Give yourself a few minutes to think about what you want to say. If you're really upset, take more time to consult with your partner and delay your response. Tell your child "This is really upsetting. I need time to think about this," or "Mom and I will talk it over. We'll let you know what we have decided." Sometimes the agony of waiting is consequence enough. It certainly allows us time to measure our response in a thoughtful way. When we speak softly but firmly, our words carry more impact.

In a seminar at New York University, Stephen Weiss, Ph.D., advises future teachers to take a time-out when they feel themselves about to lose control. In front of the children, he points to himself and says out loud, "Stephen, take a time-out." He also suggests telling the class, "I'm about to lose it. What can we do to fix this situation?"

In my first job after graduate school (Renee), I was fortunate to have a wonderful supervisor, Dr. Michael Green, director of the Child Guidance Center in Springfield, Massachusetts. Part of his role was to give parents the results of the agency's evaluation. He often had to give families a recommendation for therapy, specialized school programs and in some instances, hospitalization. At the end of their meeting with him, parents would thank him sincerely for all his help. As a naive therapist, I once asked him how he could give such bad news and have the parents accept it so well. He explained that you can say almost anything, if you do it with a smile and sincere interest. As parents, we can effectively reach our child more often with a pleasant comment or conversation than with hours of yelling!

One mother told me about an experience with her then fifteen-year-old son. He had ADD and a short fuse. All too often he had provoked her to a screaming frenzy. On this particular day, Peter wanted her to drive him to a bicycle store to get some parts for his bike. Susan had promised to take him as soon as he did his regularly assigned chores. As the day wore on and the chores had not been attempted, he continued to insist that she drive him before the store closed. When she briefly reminded him again of his responsibilities, Peter became enraged, screaming that he hated her as he swiped everything off the kitchen counter, kicked a wall and threw two chairs. Susan somehow found the wisdom and strength to say quietly, "This behavior is unacceptable." Then, she grabbed her purse and keys, left the house and went for a drive to calm herself.

When she returned a while later, the kitchen was completely cleaned up, the chores were finished and there was a note of apology on the counter. Had she stayed, most likely she and her son would have screamed at each other for some time, escalating the tension and perhaps the damage. He might have even rationalized to himself that it was okay to mess up the kitchen because Mom was being such a nasty person. Saying quietly, with restraint, "This is not acceptable" or "I am disappointed in your behavior" is far more effective and powerful than any amount of yelling.

You may be wondering about the role of explanations in order to teach your children the process of decision making. When your child asks for a decision, or there is a consequence to a behavior, it is appropriate to offer a brief description of the key points you considered in formulating your response. If your child is listening, she or he will learn what you consider to be the relevant issues. There is a good chance, however, that your child is not listening and instead is busy preparing her or his argument with you. Once you offer your rationale, there is rarely a need to repeat it. One exception might be for a child who has difficulty with auditory processing and may need to hear something several times before truly absorbing it. The explanation itself is geared toward the age of the child, becoming more sophisticated and well defined with an older child.

Here are some examples of explanations for different age groups:

**Preschooler:** With this age group, it is especially important to be brief and concise, giving one direction or request at a time. It is late afternoon, the family room floor is covered with toys and small pieces. You are trying to make dinner and get the house in some kind of order. You say to your toddler, "Let's put away the toys and make the room nice before Daddy comes home." There is no need to give a long explanation or a laundry list of all the things that have to be done. You invite cooperation rather than issue a command, and the message is direct and to the point.

**School-age:** A familiar scene: Your child comes home from school, has a snack and takes a little time to unwind. Then comes the daily reminder, "Janie, it is time to do your homework." This statement is not unexpected, especially if given at the usual time set aside for homework. It is not effective to include in the reminder a long paragraph about how she doesn't get to her work and how yesterday she took forever and then didn't have time to play. Any comments on previous behavior, lack of cooperation or anticipated trouble merely serve to set the stage for a negative interaction. A simple statement, said in a neutral tone of voice, is sufficient.

**Teenager:** The family rules stipulate that children cannot go out with friends on a school night unless it is for a school or extracurricular activity. You are tired and still finishing up some laundry. Stephen comes into the laundry room and announces, "My homework is finished, and I'm bored. I'm going over to Todd's house to help him figure out a new program on his computer." Rather than get into a dialogue about why Todd needs help or whether in fact Stephen really finished his homework, it is helpful to respond quietly, "You know the rules, no going out on a school night." If Stephen persists, answer briefly, repeating the core idea. "You know the rules."

---

 *When you ask a child to do something or answer a request, limit your response to one or two sentences.*

# 2

## Stick to the Issue

STICKING to the issue is an important communication skill in every relationship, not just between parents and children. Once we have someone's attention, it's human nature to try to squeeze in the other thirty things we have been storing up. However, that is self-defeating, because it simply does not work. You may need to have thirty separate conversations, but you will be more effective in getting your points across. If you are unhappy about something the other person did, comment—briefly—on just that one behavior. This is not an open invitation to bring up everything else we do not like. Certainly, we do not want to use statements that include the words "always" or "never."

For example, your child tells you she does not have any homework when she comes home from school. Then, just before bed, after watching television for three hours, she remembers that she has ten pages of math to do. It is tempting to speak an entire paragraph like, "Why did you lie to me? You *always* do this. I don't know why you can't be more responsible and do your work when you are supposed to. How can you get into a good college with these poor study habits? I will *never* trust you."

This approach guarantees hostility, humiliation and noncooperation. It addresses three different topics (responsibility, study habits, college) and labels the child with "always" and "never" character attacks. It is more effective to simply say, "It is now time for bed. You will have to do your work tomorrow." This is nonjudgmental, to the point and places the responsibility for problem solving back on the child. It also ensures a firm bedtime despite delay tactics.

Sometimes, in our frustration, we may express our anger by swearing or calling our child a derogatory name. There is no room in our parenting tool kit for name-calling or obscenities. Too many adults are still hurting from negative labels that were attached to them as children. Believing themselves to be lazy, stupid, selfish or cowardly, to name just a few of the labels left over from childhood memories, adults often have difficulty moving beyond these adopted self-concepts. Yet they project these same labels onto their children.

If our child came home from school and told us that the teacher had called him an idiot or a four-letter word, we would immediately protest to the teacher, principal, maybe even the board of education. If the guidance counselor tells our teenage daughter that she dresses like a "slut," we would be enraged. Yet some parents use similar terms before their child is leaving the house to go out with friends. Such a negative statement does not encourage the child to choose a different outfit—it may instead encourage the child to give an angry retort. And it definitely harms the child's sense of self.

In addition to name-calling, we also say hurtful things in times of anger or tension that are equally damaging: "I can't stand the sight of you" or "I wish you had never been born." Negative statements stay etched in a child's memory far longer and more deeply than any word of praise.

Watch our child's body language when we are yelling; the child often seems to shrink within her- or himself, the shoulders sag, the chest caves in. The child's body looks wounded or deflated. Our angry words steal our child's energy, wound our child's self-concept with a negative label and eventually erode the good, positive feelings in our relationship.

Almost any statement can be reframed in a positive, supportive way. It takes a little time to formulate a message in more helpful terms. Since we have addressed our children's appearances, let's look at some examples of how we might comment on them.

**Preschooler:** Toddlers get to a stage where they want to pick out their own clothes. We need to guide them in selecting outfits that coordinate without belittling their choices. When Amy picks out green and white striped shorts with a purple print tee shirt, we can say something like, "That's nice. I also like the white shirt with the green picture. Let's see how that would look with those shorts." We don't directly criticize the choice but try to lead them to a better match. However, if Amy is adamant that that is what she wants to wear, we can consider allowing her this choice if she is going to a friend's home or to preschool. If the occasion is special, we can be positive but firm in saying, "You can wear that to school tomorrow, but for church you need to wear a nice dress." Then offer your choice of two outfits that are appropriate, so Amy still feels she has some control and autonomy.

**School-age:** As children get older, they become more conscious of fitting in and wearing the styles of the moment. Conflict occurs when parents either can't afford the hot new sneakers that cost $150 or don't like the style—for example, dressing in black or in baggy pants. Children need some leeway in making their own choices, while parents can be mindful of budget and good taste. When we can't afford the expensive version, be brief, stick to the issue and state simply, "We don't have money to buy that shoe. I know you would really like to have the exact same shoe as your friends, but sometimes it's nice to have something a little special. Let's see what styles are available in your size for our budget." When Joey insists on wearing only the one style that you dislike, express your opinion and then try to work out a compromise. "I'm really not comfortable when you dress all in black. To me, it has a depressing, tough look. I know you want to fit in with your friends so you can select a few outfits for school, but when we go out as a family I need you to wear something different." When discussing these negotiations, make an "I" statement about your feelings. Avoid a "you" comment about your child's taste. That opens the door for perceived criticism and disapproval and may invite arguments.

Teenager: Many parents get concerned when their daughter develops breasts and a more mature figure. We worry that the sweater is too tight or cut too low or the skirt is too short. It is a big change to see our daughter become sensual in her appearance. It raises a number of issues, from when to have "the talk" to how much freedom to allow. If we're concerned about the way our daughter is dressing, we need to first look around to see how her peers are dressing. Every generation has its own look, and we need to update our visual expectations. Since teenage girls are so preoccupied with appearance to begin with, we need to tread very carefully around issues of weight, skin and clothing. Many adolescents have sobbed in our offices, relating how their parents called them a "fat pig" or a "tramp." These kinds of remarks may arise out of concern; the parents' intention may be to inspire or provoke the child to change. The result, however, is the opposite. The teen is first hurt, then furious, with the parent. Her already poor self-esteem has been confirmed, and she feels even more powerless to change. Some suggestions for a positive, supportive approach include the tools we have been discussing, as shown in the following examples.

*Statement 1.* "You look really nice tonight." If you can't say that honestly, say nothing (Zip Your Lips), or comment on some aspect that is pleasing, perhaps her hair or makeup, her choice of earrings or how pretty a certain color looks on her. (Once the girl has made her selection and is on the way out the door, we can be supportive and encouraging. This may not be the time to risk an argument or lecture about appearance or morals.)

*Statement 2.* "I am not comfortable with you wearing such a short skirt. I'd really appreciate it if you would wear the brown skirt we bought last week." (Note use of "I" statement, no attack on her choice or taste and a suggestion that might satisfy both of you. Your daughter may still insist she has nothing else to wear that fits, or that she wants to wear this outfit. Return to the suggestions in Statement 1, and let it go for now. Wait for a time when you are not arguing or she is not going out the door. Then talk about her wardrobe needs and your concerns.

Parents' concerns about appearance may also have to do with weight. When a child is overweight, she or he is well aware of this fact and probably feels pretty crummy about it. Most of the time, the best approach is to zip your lips. For example, if your son brings up his unhappiness about his weight, he may just need to vent. You may ask him to explore options with you. Draw out his feelings about it. Ask what he might like to do. Ask how you can be helpful. Offer suggestions, such as counseling, an exercise plan or buying certain groceries, but don't harp on the subject or continually bring it up. We need to take our cues from the child, who will let us know when she or he is ready to change.

Weight issues are so complicated, there are entire books devoted to the subject. The tools in this book apply to weight as well as to other areas of our parent-child interactions. There is a time for silence, a time to listen and encourage our child to talk about her or his feelings and opportunities to offer support and specific help. There is no place for name-calling, derisive remarks or constant dwelling on such sensitive topics.

Remember that children mimic and copy our behaviors. Therefore your behavior toward others serves as a role model for communication. When we talk to our partner, for example, it is extremely important to use the same positive approach and good manners we preach to our children. "Do as I say, not as I do" is not an effective modus operandi for parents. If we want children to speak respectfully to us, we need to address them—and all significant people in our lives (partner, parents, neighbors, friends)—with tact and respect.

In therapy sessions with the whole family, we observe the children speaking to the parents in the same way the parents address one another. One mother was complaining that her three teenagers, ages eighteen, fifteen and twelve, were extremely disrespectful to her. They didn't listen to anything she asked of them, and they often swore at her. Her concerns were interrupted by her husband, who cursed at her and constantly put her down.

Henry James wrote, "Three things in life are important. The first is to be kind. The second is to be kind. And the third is to be kind." When we comment on the behavior, not the person, we are being effective teachers in a firm but kind way, maximizing our children's opportunity for learning and growth.

*Comment only on the behavior at hand, not on past actions or future predictions. Avoid name-calling and the phrases "you never" and "you always."*

# 3

# *Labels Can Be Limiting*

INNOCENTLY and with all good intentions, we frequently make statements that judge and label our children's behavior.

*You are the most helpful child in the family.*

*You're going to be our financial expert some day.*

*You're going to be an artist when you grow up.*

*You are not a student.*

*You are such a klutz.*

*You are so shy.*

*You are so pretty.*

*You are so fat.*

These types of statements affect a child's self-image. They can become self-fulfilling prophesies because the child believes there is no hope of change. These labels do not encourage growth or the development of a well-rounded, integrated self. They have a heaviness and an inevitability to them.

When I (Renee) was growing up, I was stuck with several of these damaging labels. I was frequently told what a klutz I was and that I had no sense of humor. My shyness was a constant topic of conversation. When I was planning to go to college, my mother told me I needed to learn how to play bridge and make small talk or I would never have any friends. Because I saw myself as uncoordinated, I never pursued any sports activities as a child. Indeed, I was often the last one chosen for any team sports, and I did have a tendency to bump into things. However, my first boyfriend

was an avid tennis player. He decided to teach me to play. Much to my surprise, I found I was fairly good at it. I might never have sought lessons or attempted any sports without his positive encouragement.

Similarly, being told I was shy and humorless made me even more self-conscious meeting new people or in groups. I was so sure that I was boring and no one would like me that I hung back, often standing in a corner, observing the social scene rather than putting myself in it. It took me about thirty-five years to begin to relax and appreciate who I am. Some people never get to the point in their lives where they can ignore others' labels and develop their own self-appreciation. Most likely, you have some labels that were unwittingly offered to you and which may or may not have stuck.

In therapy sessions, I sometimes ask people to write all the negative adjectives they have heard or believe about themselves onto sheets of Post-it notes. They are then instructed to stick these Post-its all over their body. After they absorb the impact of this labeling experience, I suggest that these are just words, someone else's opinion or agenda. They are told they can pull off any label and see themselves in a different light.

In a variation of labeling, parents often compare one child to another in the family. "Why can't you be a good student like your big brother" implies the label of "poor student." "You are the only person in the family I can rely on to help me" puts the burden of being "the good one" on the responsible child. When that child reaches a stage where some testing or independent behavior is needed for growth, she or he may be reluctant to lose the "good child" role. This child might suppress the urge to talk back or come in a little after the curfew, losing an opportunity to feel more mature.

*To avoid labeling in its various guises, remember the concept of sticking to the issue. Comment positively and supportively on the talent, skill or behavior of the present moment.*

*"That project shows strong artistic sense."*

*"You were very helpful in cleaning the family room. I really appreciate it."*

# 4

## *Zip Your Lips*

IN THE previous chapters, we addressed the importance of being brief and sticking to the issue. There are some situations, however, where it is best to say nothing at all. Once our child has done something and we discover it after the fact, whether we agree or not, the wise course is often to zip our lips.

I (Dale) had a young woman come to see me who tearfully began the session by saying, "I hate my parents so much." As the tears rolled down her cheeks, she explained that she had a good job, her own apartment and was supporting herself. She was excited to tell her parents that she had purchased a kitten to keep her company and make her apartment feel more homey. Her parents reacted by berating her: "Why did you do that? It's stupid. Shots and food cost money, and you are barely making enough to pay your bills. You won't even be home to take care of it. You don't need a kitten, you need a boyfriend." As they continued to tell her what a poor decision she had made, she felt angry and demeaned.

Several days later, our twenty-five-year-old son called from his apartment to share his good news. He had gone to an animal shelter and "saved the life" of a small kitten. Our first reaction might have been to criticize him much as the young woman's parents just described had done. However, with the benefit of that recent experience, we said only, "That's great." We were able to share his enthusiasm so that he felt pleased about the conversation. While it may not have seemed like a good idea to us (the practical parents), the cat has turned out to be a loving companion, a source of entertainment and an opportunity for Josh to practice responsibility for another.

As you know, there are situations where a child's decision does not turn out for the best. On those occasions, our children especially need our support—and our silence. The consequence itself provides an opportunity for growth and learning. As parents, our role is to support that learning and our children's ability to handle it. "I told you so" types of statements simply rub salt in the wound.

A classic example occurs many mornings when our child is getting ready to leave for school. We have heard the weather report, so we tell our child to wear a jacket or raincoat. The child refuses, only to return after school complaining that she or he was so cold all day or got soaked on the way home. Instead of reminding our child that we may know best, an "I told you so" statement only causes the child to feel demeaned, embarrassed and hostile toward us. We need to remember that good judgment comes from learning, and learning often comes from bad judgment.

Here are some examples of instances where we can zip our lips.

**Preschooler:** You are at the park on a beautiful sunny day. You notice that Sam is climbing too high on the monkey bars. You call out to him that it is dangerous to go so high; he will fall off and get hurt. As you start to move to pull him back, he climbs higher, loses his balance and falls to the ground, crying. In your concern and your anger, you want to scold him for not listening. But all he needs is a quick inspection to see if there is serious injury and a big hug to reassure him. When you refrain from a reprimand, you allow him to draw his own conclusion, to feel your comfort and support and turn an unhappy moment into a learning experience.

**School-age:** Andrea has a tendency to be very controlling when she has friends over. You have talked with her in the past about this behavior and how it affects her friends. Today, she is being especially bossy, and after a short time together, her friend starts to cry and leaves to walk home. Soon after, Andrea is complaining to you that she is bored. Resist the temptation to remind her of her behavior or your previous warnings. You can simply acknowledge her feelings with a nod or a look that says, "Oh well," and allow her to deal with her thoughts and feelings.

**Teenager:** George has a major research paper due in two days. It was assigned six weeks ago, and you have suggested periodically that he should get started. Now he is panicked because he has done very little work, and he is asking you to help him search for information and write the report. It is so tempting to berate him for not starting earlier, for being disorganized. He is well aware that he should have been working on this all along and that you reminded him to do so. Bringing up these issues would only exacerbate touchy feelings and deplete valuable energy that he needs to get to work. Stick to the issue. Calmly state whether you are available at all to help in this last-minute effort. Or suggest that he should get started and see how much he can complete. Then, no matter how hard this might be, disappear, back off and *zip your lips*. What a great learning opportunity for George! Even if this is the fifteenth time this has happened, he is learning something about procrastination and lack of planning.

**Adult:** Mr. T. has a long commute over busy highways. He usually arrives around 7:00 PM in time for dinner with the family. Tonight he arrives 90 minutes late. Everyone is worried. Rather than berate him for being so late and spoiling dinner, Mrs. T. chooses to say, "I'm glad you are home safely. We were getting concerned." Mr. T. is already tired and frazzled. He appreciates being warmly received rather than chastised for circumstances beyond his control.

*Once a child's decision has been made or an action has occurred, the best response is silence. Allow children to experience the consequences of their own choices, instead of saying, "I told you so." Zip your lips. Silence encourages more positive feelings with our child, and it frees the child to learn from the experience.*

# 5

## Lecture #537, or How to Win Attention and Influence Children

IN OUR well-meaning attempts to influence and teach our children, we repeat ourselves thousands of times. I first noticed this when my children teased me with, "Here comes lecture #537—you know, the one about responsibility and trust." Chances are, they could repeat verbatim what I intended to say. Therefore, this chapter is about telling a good story *once*, using humor where appropriate, and referring back to the story in summary as needed. Do not repeat the whole thing unless you want to sound senile and guarantee an absentee audience. We hear ourselves doing it and probably rationalize that the more children hear something, the better they will incorporate it.

Children need to repeat certain behaviors in order to learn from the experience and fully integrate the knowledge gained. Thus young children want to hear their favorite story over and over. Older children may wait until the last minute to finish a report even though his or her previous experiences caused stress and a finished product that was less than her or his best work. After we have said "no" to a request, our child continues to try and change our answer. It is the child's need to repeat behaviors. However, if we reiterate the same answer or lengthy lecture too often, we put ourselves out of the conversational ballgame. Our child simply tunes us out or views the repetition as an open invitation to continue to argue in order to wear us out.

Kids learn more from our example than our words. If you really mean that something might happen if they leave their bicycle outside in the rain or at school, you may need to let natural consequences make your point rather than repeating your message every time the bicycle is outdoors. No one says you have to replace a lost or stolen bicycle or fix a damaged one. Explain your position once, and let the child experience the consequences of not listening. Your brief words will take on more meaning than a thousand reminders!

Children love to hear about their parents when they were little or about how they met. When told in the form of stories in a relaxed atmosphere, these stories can fascinate children with the ways of a different era and the behavior of a youthful mom, dad, grandparent or other relative. On the other hand, when we offer a lecture about our deprived childhood or difficult life, kids are turned off and annoyed. Many parents find themselves buying their children expensive clothes and equipment, then reminding the recipient that "I never even had my own bedroom when I was little.

You are so lucky." Telling children they should be more appreciative will not make them so. It's important that they learn about our history and that our parents worked hard to provide their family with a simple life. But this information is best absorbed in a neutral or enjoyable family context, not as a scolding or lecture. Children really can't appreciate what they have until they are older, perhaps after they have been on their own for a while and have gained some perspective.

When you must convey something important to your child, you can avoid the need to repeat yourself by making eye contact or physical contact. Frequently we yell something to a child in a different room or say something while she or he is watching TV, talking on the phone or using the computer. We then get exasperated because she or he does not respond. Later, we get annoyed when the child screams something from another part of the house. So before you speak, make sure you have your child's attention. Ask her or him to look at you while you are talking. Then you can better gauge her or his responsiveness. Avoid delivering messages through another person. Asking a brother or sister to convey a message to a sibling is asking for that message to get lost or misinterpreted in the translation.

Finally, pay attention to your tone of voice. Keep it light, and use humor when possible without being demeaning or sarcastic. When someone yells at me, I get anxious and often miss the whole message. The same is true with children. They learn quite early to tune us out just by looking at our expression or hearing a certain edge in our voice. If we want our message to be received, we should try to keep our tone of voice normal and pleasant. You may be thinking, "Yes, but this is so hard to do." True, speaking calmly often goes against our natural instincts. But, like any job, if you want to be good at it, you have to make some efforts. If yelling worked, there would be no need for a different approach. Try to take a deep breath or catch yourself before you respond to your child. Think about the phrasing and intent.

Each time you work on staying calm and collected, you will get improved results, which in turn encourages you to continue this new approach. Eventually, it does seem more natural and requires less effort. If, however, we are really angry, it is important for our child to see that we are upset. That is part of our message. It would be confusing to say sweetly, "Janie dear, I am a little concerned that you strangled the cat."

We need not be surprised if our son or daughter does not take our advice. In fact, it is often more likely to be accepted if we offer an *opinion* rather than an *order*. When our child misbehaves or has a problem, we tend to either tell the child what to do about it or tell a long story about how "that happened to me, and I handled it like this," implying she or he should do the same. People learn by experience. So, as much as we want to protect our children and give them the benefit of our experiences, they may still choose to hit their head against the same brick wall. Our words can be helpful by planting a seed of an idea, giving an opinion to consider or as validation after the fact. Instead of taking our children's choices as a rejection or a signal to speak louder and longer, we can respect their need to discover life on their own terms. We can be there for support and damage control.

Let's look at some examples.

**Preschooler:** You notice Michael, age three, hitting his sister, Cynthia, age one. This has been happening more often as Cynthia has become more mobile. You have told Michael a number of times that hitting is not allowed.

He has been placed on the time-out stool each time to reinforce the point that hitting will not be tolerated. Once again, you go over, take him to the time-out stool and state simply that he needs to stay there for three minutes for hitting his sister. He does not need to hear the whole spiel about hitting. It only prolongs the consequence, gives him a chance to argue with you and distract the focus, creating more tension.

**School-age:** Meredith comes home from school very upset. She says that her best friend was whispering about her at the lunch table, telling the other girls not to be friends with her anymore. Of course you are hurt and upset for your daughter. Perhaps you have even had a similar experience in your life. Your daughter tearfully asks you, "What should I do?" Beware of this potential trap. In our desire to comfort our child and share our years of acquired wisdom, we naturally want to jump in with suggestions of what to do or say.

Instead, we suggest that you ask about her ideas on dealing with the situation. Or you might inquire about her feelings as this was happening. "How did you feel when they were talking about you?" "What did you do with your feelings?" You could also brainstorm with her about what might be causing her friend's behavior. If you give her advice too quickly, it may backfire. You may be surprised to hear your daughter on the phone later that evening laughing with this same friend. On the other hand, she may come back to you in anger and say that trying your advice made things worse. Now she is angry, not with the friend but with you. Don't attempt to defend your advice. She needs support for her feelings, not a logical discussion. Try commenting, "I'm sorry it didn't go well. You must be really upset." Give her space to vent her frustration or hurt. Omit the lecture about her choice of friends and the argument about whether or not your suggestion was appropriate.

**Teenager:** As a normal part of adolescence, teens may experience some depression. It may last for an hour, a day or longer. Usually it is transient and works itself out. Many parents try to "cheer up" their teen by saying, "You shouldn't feel that way. What do you have to be depressed over? You don't know how easy you have it. When I was your age I didn't have a computer, a car, nice clothes. I had to work every day after school to help my folks. That was depressing!" This approach is guaranteed to anger your teen and discourage any further discussion. It's better to acknowledge the child's feelings and ask open-ended questions if you want your child to confide in you and feel comfortable. You can't solve or fix the sadness, but just listening supportively may be the most helpful intervention you can offer.

---

 *When we repeat the same story or advice, it loses effectiveness and alienates the listener.*

# 6

# "Why?" Doesn't Work

PICTURE THIS: You're on the phone, talking to a friend. Usually this is an open invitation to your child to interrupt and demand your attention. This time, however, you are pleased that your toddler seems to be playing nicely on his own. After you get off the phone, you go upstairs and find that he has decorated his walls with permanent Magic Markers. The first, natural response is to scream in anguish, "Why did you do that?" In your calmer, rational moments you can laugh at the question. What did you expect your four-year-old to say? "I wanted to get your attention"? "I was mad at you because you didn't let me have another cookie"? "I plan to be the next Picasso, and I'm starting my cubist period early"?

Young children, for the most part, truly do not know why they do what they do. They do not yet have the self-awareness or the vocabulary to be able to identify their motives. Often, even older children with some of these developing skills honestly don't know what propelled them to take apart a VCR, steal a package of gum from the

supermarket or beat up on their little brother. It is usually a waste of time to ask why. It is equally nonproductive to ask, "Did you do this?" Though we want our children to learn to take responsibility for their actions, a child's first response is usually to deny guilt in order to save face and avoid punishment. It takes many years to learn that the consequences are less severe when they own up to their behavior than when they lie.

Bill Cosby had a wonderful routine in his comedy act many years ago. Recalling his childhood, he remembered a time when he and his brother were upstairs jumping on the bed. They were having a great time, giggling and shrieking. Their dad was downstairs watching television and heard the thumping on the floorboards above. He stomped up the stairs, flung open the door and glared at the boys. They stopped jumping at the sight of their father's furious look. "Were you jumping?" he asked. The frightened boys looked at each other, stood as still as they could, looked at Dad and replied, "Nope." He told them he would beat them twice, once for jumping on the bed, a second time for telling a fib. Even caught in the act, children often will try to wiggle out of a punishment by denying culpability.

But how, without asking "Why?" or "Did you do it?," do we deal with misbehavior in a way that teaches responsibility, sets limits and leaves our child's self-esteem intact? Let's go back to the discovery of the Magic Markers. You could say, "I see you have been decorating your walls." Your child may look at you anxiously, knowing on some level that his drawing was not appropriate, but he may also have some pride in the creation. It would be helpful to say something such as, "John, thanks for letting me talk on the phone without interrupting. And I really like your coloring, but you know painting on the walls is not allowed. Next time I'm on the phone, let's find something fun for you to do."

You could talk together about either cleaning up the mess or living with it. Then suggest acceptable places to color and be creative. Sometimes we think that approach does not sound angry enough. Our child won't get the message that she or he had better not do this again. The fact is, *children do get the message*. They know what we expect from them. But they also need to experiment, to test, to see where the boundaries are. And they do not learn from a single reprimand or experience. So they will do it again no matter how loudly we yell or how hard we punish. Handle situations in a way that teaches what is right but also allows them to retain their dignity and to respect us, their most important teachers.

**School-age:** When you pick up Alex, age nine, at school, you mention that you have to stop at the grocery store. Rather than his usual complaint, he seems surprisingly agreeable. He disappears for a little while, then meets up with you at the check out counter. Later, at home, you hear him tell his friend that he got the neatest video today. Knowing that he didn't have any money to buy a video at the store, and you didn't get it for him, you go into his room and see the freshly opened tape. The ineffective response is to yell, to lecture about stealing and to ask why. What could he say? I wanted it? I thought it would be fun to steal, to see if I could get away with it? Rather, in the context of effective communication, you might simply say, "I am disappointed in you. Get your jacket. We are taking this back to the store." Alex knows that he did something wrong. He expects you to be upset with him. Chances are he feels disappointed in himself on some level. It is consequence enough to live with your silent disapproval and to face the store manager when returning the stolen item. You are acting responsibly, and he will learn from your example.

Teenager: Janine is supposed to come home after school, take the dog for a walk and do her homework. She is also expected to call you at work to let you know she's home. One day she calls and seems in a hurry to get off the phone. After hanging up, you remember an instruction to get dinner started and try to call her right back. There is no answer. You try her again several times in the course of an hour but she is not home. Finally, you call her best friend's house, and sure enough, she is there. If you ask her, "Did you go home after school?," it gives her the opening to lie to you. Were you to question why she didn't go home, it shifts the focus away from the fact that she did not live up to her responsibilities and on to her motivation. Instead, keep the conversation focused on the main issue by saying, "I see that you ignored our agreement to come home after school and walk the dog." Depending on your agreement, a consequence may already have been stipulated, so you would add, "Therefore you can't go out with your friends one day of the weekend." If there had never been an agreement on a potential consequence, depending on the age and maturity of your daughter and on her general reliability, you may ask her to suggest a consequence or negotiate together what may follow. There is no need to expend energy on a long lecture about trust and responsibility or previous offenses.

Focus on this behavior, the consequence, and then let the topic end.

There are times when you will not know which of your children is the culprit. I remember one night when we had left our children, ages eight, seven, and three, with a babysitter. When we came home, we noticed a pile of paint shavings on the carpet next to the door frame into our son's bedroom. Someone had picked off several inches of paint from the molding. The next day we gathered the three together and asked the obvious question, "Which one of you did this?" We were faced with three blank stares, as if they did not have a clue what we were talking about. We told them to think about it, and until we found the one responsible, all three would be denied television for the rest of the weekend. To this day, we do not know who did it. Rather than accuse a child falsely (even though we had a strong suspicion based on previous history) we accused no one. In a way, we appreciated their loyalty to each other.

Group consequences can be effective. When group consequences are applied, the siblings may pressure the guilty party to confess. They may exert their own kind of punishment on that sibling or let it be known that they won't cover up the next time.

*When you know your child misbehaved, don't ask, "Why?" or "Did you?" Comment simply on the behavior, express your feelings and state the consequence.*

# 7

# How to Say "No"
# —and Mean It

IN THE seventies and eighties, as a counter to a more authoritarian approach to parenting, parents were encouraged to tell their children *why* they were answering in a certain way. Of course, it is helpful at times to share the reasoning behind a decision. Hearing the information that leads to a decision helps children learn the process of decisionmaking. However, when we find ourselves repeating the explanation for the third time, now in a more exasperated tone, saying, "I told you before," that is the warning sign that we have talked too much.

When your child asks permission to do something, buy something or go somewhere, think about your response. Take as much time as you need, within reason, to consider your answer. Some requests are simple, and we know immediately what our response will be. Other requests need more time to think through. The requests often come when we are busy or cranky, or feel we have already done so much for our child. Our knee-jerk reaction is to say no. If we were to delay a response and think about the ramifications, we might have a different reaction or find that we need more information. Once you make your decision, however, communicate it briefly, make direct eye contact and ask your child for confirmation that she or he understands.

An effective approach entails answering your child once, maybe twice with a younger child or one who has trouble listening and processing verbal information. If the child asks a second or third time, however, some appropriate replies would be:

> *"We already discussed this."*
>
> *"You know the answer."*
>
> *"The subject is closed."*

Or ask the child to repeat what you said as a way of clarifying whether in fact she or he understood. Such responses serve the purpose of avoiding arguments and keeping the discussion brief.

This approach also helps to teach your child how to get your attention in positive ways rather than through the negative tactic of engaging you in prolonged arguments. Select one of the above phrases, or a *brief* variation, depending on the circumstance and the personality of the child. These key phrases need to be followed by *action*. Children do not always respond to our words. They do respond to our behavior.

Your first action after making a decision is to be deaf to further questioning. This can be demonstrated by a shrug, no response at all or pointing to your ears and then shrugging, as if to say, "I can't hear you." It is always helpful when you plan to improve your parenting to announce in advance what the new strategy will be. This gives the child notice that a change is afoot. It then becomes crucial to stick to this approach, otherwise your child has no reason to take you seriously.

If the child is really persistent, or has learned to argue long enough so that you cave in, an alternate response, after stating one of the key phrases above, is "We've talked about this before. I'm not going to change my mind. You can continue to bring this up but I'm not going to respond." Here is how it might flow.

**Preschooler:** You have to go to the toy store because Alyssa, age four, is invited to a birthday party. She starts to pester you to buy her everything she sees. You tell her, "We aren't buying you a toy today. We are only here to buy your friend's present." Then try to distract her with a silly song, give her a hug for helping you find the gift or make up a game of finding something in the store. If she persists in demanding something for herself, you can repeat one more time, "Not today," or pretend to be deaf. She will get the message.

**School-age:** You have picked up Amy and Tommy from school and have to stop at the drugstore and the cleaners. In the car, they ask if you will take them to McDonald's for dinner. You explain that it will be too early for dinner when you finish your errands, and you will all be having dinner at home. Amy complains that you never take them to McDonald's anymore, and she never gets to do what she wants. Tommy chimes in that he hates your dinner. After a busy day, you are starting to get irritable and develop a headache. The old way would have been to argue that you took them to McDonald's two weeks ago. You realize that the response would invite further arguing and prolong the conversation. Now you wisely say, "The subject is closed," and prepare to listen—without responding—to their complaints. Should they persist in repeating the question, you will now shrug your shoulders and use the selective deafness approach. The children will soon get the message that it is fruitless to argue this point. They may move on to the next request ("Can I have a friend over when we get home?" or "Will you take me to the video store?"). When needed, you can continue to practice saying "no" in a brief, effective way. Sometimes children make a string of unrealistic requests, particularly if they are unhappy or bored. There is no magic ratio of positive/negative responses. We need not feel guilty that we have denied their last three requests, so we say "yes" to the fourth one. Each request needs to be evaluated on its own merit.

Teenager: Matthew, fourteen, wants to go to his first rock concert. He can get a ride with his friend's brother who just got his license. It is in a sports arena one hour away. You tell him you will talk it over with your partner and get back to him. He starts to pressure you for an answer right away because his friend is going that afternoon to buy the tickets. You reply, "This is an important decision, and I want to give it careful consideration. Both parents need to agree, so I just can't answer you now." He will continue to bother you, insisting on an answer. You can reply quietly but firmly, "If you continue to pester me, the answer will be no. I will get back to you as soon as possible." There is no reason to continue to answer. Later, after both parents have considered, you let him know your decision. Obviously, if the answer is yes, the discussion will focus on the details of the plan. But if your answer is no, try explaining the factors that went into your decision and what alternatives you might offer (for example, a concert closer to home, parents driving, going when he is older). Be prepared for persistent protests. When he challenges your reasoning, state, "Matthew, we thought it over carefully, and we feel strongly about it. I know you are disappointed." There is no room here to revive the discussion. It respects his feelings and his right to be disappointed. It also lets him know you care about him. Further attempts on his part to go over it again can be met with a simple statement, "We already talked about it" or "I'm not going to change my mind."

Is there any room to reconsider once we have said no? We don't want to cave in just because our child wears us down with persistent questioning. But we do want to teach our children to be assertive and speak up for what is important to them. So we might rethink our position if we answered out of haste or irritation. We may also listen to our child's reasoning and if the plan or needs are valid, change our reply. We can just be honest and say, "I've thought it over and decided that you can go to the concert under the following conditions."

When our child bombards us with requests, it is helpful to step back from the situation and try to discern any underlying cause. For example, one of the children may be sick and require a lot of attention. Another child may feel neglected or unloved and makes demands on our time as a way of testing whether we really care. When the real agenda is the child's underlying emotions and not self-centered requests, we respond to the feelings involved.

While the child may deny experiencing these feelings or overtly reject our reassurances, she or he has, on some level, heard our words and been comforted. Try saying to the child, "Sweetie, you have been asking for a lot of things lately. Maybe you are feeling that you don't get enough attention." Pause to see what kind of response you get. If the child agrees with your observation, you can encourage her or him to talk about those feelings. The child may deny such feelings out of embarrassment or a reluctance to talk about it. Then you might want to add, "It was just an idea I had. I love you very much, and maybe we could think of a way to spend some time together."

*The importance of following through once you have made a "No" reply is crucial.* This alone will save hours of extended arguing. Remember, children learn by repetition. If they have learned from experience that arguing and nagging will wear you down and get them their way, they will continue this behavior. As we become more skilled in saying "no" effectively, both in words and actions, kids will realize that persistent requests won't work. They will learn to accept our decision much sooner.

*When we make a decision and say "no" to a request, give the reasons, if appropriate, then end the conversation. Say what you mean, then mean what you say. That is how we establish credibility.*

# 8

## *The "You Can Do It" Approach*

AS CHILDREN grow older and more capable, an important tool for building their self-esteem is the "You can do it" approach. Sometimes children give up too quickly on a new task or skill, such as learning to tie shoes or selecting an outfit. Too often children will ask the parent, "What should I do?" when looking for help with an assignment, a problem with a friend or a decision about whether to sign up for an activity. Our natural tendency, knowing ourselves to be older and wiser, is to offer our suggestions. Isn't that what our child is seeking? Shouldn't we give our guidance and knowledge? Not necessarily. Instead, we may want to turn the question back to our child.

There are two major reasons why providing an answer is not necessarily the most helpful response. First, we give the child an unspoken but powerful message that she or he really is incapable of figuring it out. This message is the opposite of empowerment, and in a subtle way it is demeaning, although that certainly is not our intent. Second, our answer may lead to an argument. Most likely we have all had the experience of providing an appropriate suggestion to our child in response to a request for help, only to be rejected: "That is a stupid idea, that won't work, that's not what the teacher wants." We feel angry that our child asked for help and now won't accept it. Some of my angriest moments with our children occurred while trying to "help" them with their written assignments. Since I had been an English major, I was sure my expert advice would be most welcome. I would be moved by their tears and insistence that they just could not think of a topic. I suggested what I thought were wonderful ideas, none of which was acceptable. The result was frustration on both sides.

When the request centers around a school assignment or interpersonal issue, ask your child to brainstorm with you: "What do you think?" "What would happen if you . . .?" "What are some other possibilities? Think about what has worked in the past." "Have you thought about . . .?" These phrases throw the responsibility back onto the child. The ideas become the child's own, so she or he will be more receptive to them. We can guide the discussion by our questions. If we feel strongly that the child is not coming up with an appropriate idea, we can offer an opinion either directly or by asking, "Have you thought about . . .?" Then back off, stressing that the child can review the alternatives and make a wise choice.

"You can do it" is the ultimate vote of confidence. It is the most powerful phrase in your parenting vocabulary, with the exception of "I love you." There will be so many times when children beg us to make their decision. Beware of this trap. If, in fact, we review the options and possible consequences together, most children will be able to make sound choices. We are teaching them our values. They pick up what we want them to do even if we don't say it, and they can sort it out. Even if we do not agree with their decision (unless it is dangerous), we can *zip our lips* and let them learn from their mistakes. If our daughter decides to watch television all evening and not do her homework, in most cases we need to let her suffer tomorrow's consequences. One exception might be a child who has great difficulty concentrating or organizing time and needs the parent to provide more structure.

"You can do it" can also work when children are learning a new skill. Your toddler may be learning to tie her or his shoes. Still, the child asks you for help. You might suggest that she or he make the "bunny ears" and you will do the rest until the child can do the whole thing alone. Encourage and allow young children to do as much as they are capable of doing. Then zip your lips about the way it is done, praising only the fact that they tried to accomplish a new, difficult task. Here are some examples of ways to do just that.

Preschooler: Tonya, age five, has suddenly been waking up during the night with scary dreams. She started coming into her parents' bedroom, wanting to get into bed with them because she is frightened. Mom wants to let Tonya climb in so she can go back to sleep, but she fears it will become a routine. Tonya does not adjust to change readily, and once she starts a new routine, it would be even harder to change again. So instead, Mom rouses herself, walks Tonya back to bed, tucks her in and sits on the edge of the bed for a few minutes. She pats her arm and talks softly to her. "Tonya, you've been sleeping every night in your own bed, and nothing has happened. You are a big girl, and you can stay in your room and fall asleep. There is nothing to be afraid of. Dad and I are in the next room if you really needs us, but you are such a brave girl." Tonya will cry, protest that she is not brave and she can't go to sleep. Many parents give in at this point, because it is easy and they are too tired to argue. Remember, encouraging Tonya to stay in her room is an invitation to grow, to conquer a difficult obstacle and move past it. To bring her into your bed is infantilizing and weakens her self-esteem. So when Tonya protests, one approach is to quietly reaffirm your faith in her to deal with this. Let her know how long you are prepared to stay and that you will just be down the hall if she really needs you. Be prepared to walk her back to her own bed a number of times. She—and you—will get through this and once again enjoy a good night's sleep.

**School-age:** Andrew has been begging his parents to let him take tennis lessons. Finally they agree and sign him up for a series of group lessons at the local YMCA. After two lessons, he comes home, face flushed, looking as if he might burst into tears.

*Andrew:* I hate tennis. I'm never going back there.

*Parent:* What do you mean, you aren't going back? I paid for eight classes because you insisted on taking lessons. That's throwing good money away. You have to go back. (This could be the start of a major argument unless the parent shifts the focus.)

*Andrew:* You can't make me go there.

*Parent:* I'm really puzzled. You seemed enthusiastic last week. What happened today?

*Andrew:* This kid George thinks he's so great. He told me I was a loser and he wouldn't be partners with me.

*Parent:* Boy, that's rough. I can see why you were upset. Then what happened?

*Andrew:* Another kid came over and said he would be my partner, but I still don't want to go back there.

*Parent:* Andrew, I know it will be hard to face George when he is so rude, but you really wanted to learn tennis, and it would be a lot of fun for the family to play together, so I hope you can stick it out. You remember when there was someone in your kindergarten class who used to tease all the kids, and you learned how to ignore him. I bet you can do that with George!

When a child undertakes a new activity, it's important not to let her or him bail out too quickly. You can't begin to enjoy something until you develop some level of skill, which takes time. Kids are often discouraged by their own lack of skill, especially if they compare themselves to another child. They can also be discouraged by an insensitive coach who only lets the better players stay in a game or by teasing from peers. When we support and encourage our child's effort to overcome the frustration and see an activity to its natural resolution (the end of the lessons or the season), we are showing our faith that they have the inner strength and character to deal with adversity. Isn't that what we want to teach our children?

**Teenager:** Zachary really wants to get a job after school to save money for a car. He is uncomfortable walking up to strangers to ask for a job. He asks his dad to talk to a family friend who owns a store in the mall. It would be easy for the father to approach the friend, but it is more helpful to encourage Zach to do it himself. Dad can offer to drive him over and wait in the car; he can role-play with Zach, rehearsing how to ask for a position; he can review with Zach the strengths and skills that would qualify him for the job. Finally, Dad can give him a pep talk, reassuring Zach that he will be able to get the words out and present himself well. While the "You can do it" approach may leave Zach anxious, it also empowers him. This may be the first of many job interviews over a lifetime. What better opportunity to get over the first-time jitters than with a supportive parent behind him!

**New College Student:** Daria called home from college after two days, crying. She hated it there and wanted her parents to come and get her. When her parents tried to inquire what was wrong, she mumbled through her tears, "everything." Her roommate was weird, no one on her floor seemed friendly and already she could tell all her classes were too hard for her. This scenario is not that uncommon, whether it is a younger child going to sleepaway camp or a young adult going off to college.

Many parents panic and feel they have to retrieve their unhappy child right away. The "You can do it" approach suggests a different tack. Daria's parents might offer to call her later that evening or the next day to see how she is doing. They could negotiate a visit in the near future if the school is not too far away. Most importantly, they need to express their confidence that their daughter will succeed in this new setting. Children need encouragement to realize that it takes time to adjust to any new situation. Daria may feel that "everyone else" is doing just fine and has found friends, but that is not realistic. Mom and Dad can help Daria consider various options to meet people and get through each day. But to allow her to bail out so quickly would cheat her of an opportunity to reach inside and find her own strength. Once she has adjusted, she will feel tremendously empowered and pleased with herself. Even if she eventually decides to transfer to another school, she can feel confident to face another challenge.

Goethe wrote, "If I accept you as you are, I will make you worse; however, if I treat you as though you are what you are capable of becoming, I help you become that."

*Rather than answer a question or take over a child's struggling effort, we empower and encourage our children by saying, "You can do it. I have faith in you" or "Do as much as you can, then I'll help with the rest." This approach builds a child's self-esteem and creates a positive feeling toward the parent.*

# 9

## When to Join the Opposition

ALL CHILDREN love to argue some of the time. To an extent, this is important to their development in practicing negotiation and assertiveness skills. Some children are more confrontational by nature and argue most of the time. It is emotionally draining for parents and children when arguments are the main vehicle of communication. To short-circuit this pattern, try joining the opposition. By this we mean that when your child makes a statement that is wrong, exaggerated or overtly challenging, you simply *agree in a neutral tone of voice.*

*Child:* You never do anything for me.

*Parent (Option 1):* You're right.

*Parent (Option 2):* Really?

*Parent (Option 3):* You're right. I never let you have a friend over or make your favorite dinner or buy you new clothes when you need them or take you to piano. It's true, I never do anything for you.

*Child:* No, that's not what I meant. I just wanted you to. . . .

Option 3 works only if done with a light touch! The point is not to make fun of the child but to *emphasize the exaggeration of the statement.* When this is done with *kindness* and *humor,* it brings the focus back to the real issue and defuses a potentially explosive situation. Our child can laugh with us as long as our tone of voice is playful, not mocking, patronizing or demeaning.

Sometimes a child starts an argument because she or he is unhappy or tense about something. The child may not even realize what that something is or may be very aware and may need to talk about it but cannot bring it up directly. One mother had really reached her limit of patience with her fourteen-year-old daughter, who was in a very bratty phase. Her daughter seemed to be attacking her in every interaction. One day she tried a different approach when her daughter came home from school.

*Mom:* Hi, how was your day?

*Cindy:* Terrible, and you look really dumb in those jeans.

*Mom:* Boy, you look like you could use a hug. (Goes over and gives her daughter a hug even though Cindy stiffens up.) Why don't you sit down and I'll make you a cup of cocoa?

This mom was surprised to report that her daughter not only sat down but began to tell her about an encounter in the lunchroom when one of her friends made a mean remark about her in a loud voice. They were able to talk about how hurt Cindy felt instead of battling about appearances, which would have escalated into a harangue about other things. If we do not take the oppositional bait but instead offer love and support, at the least we may avert an argument; at best, we may have a meaningful conversation about some things bothering our child.

Here is another way to deal with a defiant statement or obviously poor choice:

> *Child:* Well, I don't care what you say. I'm not going to do my homework. I'm watching the ball game.
>
> *Parent:* That's up to you, but if I were you, I'd think about that choice more carefully. You know that if you don't get your homework done, there will be a consequence.

You can state the consequence if it is a known rule or leave it open-ended for the child to contemplate. By not forbidding the child to do what she or he wants, you are avoiding a power struggle. You are still conveying the appropriate behavior. In using one of these approaches to join the opposition, you avoid a confrontation ("No, you can't!" "Yes, I Can!") and defuse the tension. You also increase your chances of learning what is creating the tension. You can give more positive responses so that in the course of a day, you are not saying more angry words than neutral or loving statements.

**Preschooler:** It's time to leave your friend's house where the mothers were chatting while the children were playing. You tell Michael you will be leaving in a few minutes. He starts to protest that he wants to stay. When you get your coat on, you give him his jacket. He throws it on the floor and tells you he won't put it on. You say calmly that you are leaving and start for the door. He puts on his jacket and follows you out. Often young children exercise their voice and refuse to do something, only to turn around and do it if we step back for a few minutes.

**School-age:** Dina's job is to walk the dog when she gets home from school. The dog has been in the house all day and really needs to go out. You remind Dina, who is talking on the phone to a friend she just saw in school, that Pooch needs to go out. She tells you she will do it in a few minutes. Let her know that may be too late, but then she can clean up the mess if Pooch doesn't make it until then. Then turn aside or leave the room. Chances are she will come through. No one likes to jump right up when they are told to do something. Delaying the response allows the listener to choose the response rather than feel controlled by another. It is also a way of saving face, which we will discuss in a later chapter.

**Teenager:** I (Dale) was seeing a family with a twelve-year-old boy who refused to talk to them. He carried a pad of paper and communicated through writing. He had been suspended from school for fighting another student. The parents warned me that he wouldn't talk. I decided to go with the flow. I wrote on a pad of paper, "Are we talking verbally out loud or in writing? Your choice." Here is the correspondence.

*Walter:* You can speak if you want to.

*Dale:* No, let's keep it balanced.

*Walter:* What do you want to talk about?

*Dale:* Your anger.

*Walter:* Okay.

*Dale:* Your loss of control, the trouble in school.

*Walter:* Oh. (Then there was a long pause. He didn't write anything else.)

*Dale:* (After waiting a minute or two) I love the silence. Do you?

*Walter:* I was kicked off the bus for five school days because I punched a kid in the chest.

*Dale:* What are you trying to tell us with your behavior in school?

*Walter:* (He describes the fight and explains that the other boy had assaulted him earlier.)

*Dale:* Do you want to stay in that school?

*Walter:* Yes. I know some of my behavior will have to improve.

By joining his oppositional behavior and writing together, I was able to help Walter take responsibility for his behavior. He didn't feel defensive but accepted. With this support, he was able to talk more about his anger, recognizing that by not talking, he was trying to contain his feelings. They were then able to talk (write) together about other ways to express feelings that were more appropriate.

*With a child who is argumentative, use a variety of techniques to avoid the call to debate: agree in an exaggerated but kind way; look beyond angry words to address underlying feelings; go with the flow; state the consequences of a refusal.*

# 10

## The 1-2-3 Method

ONE OF the most common complaints from parents is that they cannot get their children to do what they want, when they want it done. In order to understand this pattern, we need to try and put ourselves in our children's place. Do we like to be told to do something, and do it *now*? I (Renee) know I do not respond well to that kind of order. Further, what is important to us is usually not on our child's list of priorities. We may want a clean, orderly home, but that is generally not important to our children.

When we want something done, we can ask for our child's help in a way that invites cooperation and makes the child feel needed and important. Remember to begin your request with "please" and later thank your child for her or his help. This encourages further cooperation, demonstrates good manners (without lecturing) and creates an atmosphere of good feelings. I remember going for a walk in the park with friends. When we came to an intersection, Gerri turned to her five-year-old and said, "David, I need you to hold my hand while we cross the street." David, a typically rambunctious child offered his hand without protest, and I was struck by the gentle yet firm way Gerri addressed him. A variation of this approach is to say, "Michelle, would you please take the clothes out of the dryer and fold them for me? I need your help so I can finish getting dinner ready!" Once the clothes are folded, you comment, "I appreciate your help. I couldn't get everything done without you."

These approaches sound great on paper, and they really do work in real life—most of the time. However, there are occasions when our child is happily absorbed in an activity. Our child doesn't want to be helpful, at least not in our time frame, and acts as if she or he didn't even hear us. Then we reach into our parental tool kit and pull out the 1–2–3 method. The 1–2–3 method is a simple technique. The first step in implementing it is to explain to your children what you expect (since it's important to let them know in advance the new approach). Explain that you will begin counting slowly, and if you get to 3, they will not be happy. At this point, children will want to know what will happen if . . . ? You can be vague and ominous, as in, "Believe me, you really don't want to find out." This approach is reminiscent of our mother reaching for the wooden spoon or our father starting to take off his belt. We may never have gotten hit, but the threat was enough for us to shape up. It is okay for your children to be a little afraid of you and of what you might do. Better to have an air of mystery than for your children to think you are pushovers and to be able to predict how you will react. In fact, we may have conditioned them to think of us as ineffective.

Your response can also be very specific if the outcome is a natural consequence of the behavior, such as going to bed without a story if the child dawdles too long. How to select consequences will be addressed in Chapter 12. After you ask the child to do something and she or he does not respond, you slowly start to count. Your child needs to know up front that if you reach the number 3 and she or he has not begun to move, there is a consequence. That knowledge is crucial to the effectiveness of this method. Here are some examples of the 1–2–3 method at work.

**Preschooler:** One couple was having a lot of trouble getting their very active four-year-old ready for bed. She delayed at every opportunity. Finally, they told her about the 1–2–3 method and explained that if she dawdled, she would no longer get her story time. When she refused to get out of the bathtub, they started counting. When she lingered too long on the toilet, they got to number 2. They were able to decrease the bedtime preparations from 45 minutes to 15, giving the child a half hour more of needed rest and creating a more pleasant send-off to bedtime. Naturally, she tested her parents a few times to see what would happen if she waited until they got to 3. She screamed in protest one night when she did not get her bedtime story and cried herself to sleep. The next night she was much more cooperative.

**School-age:** Julie loved to talk with her friends on the phone. It was a constant source of friction because the rest of the family also needed to use the phone. Every night her parents would yell at Julie to get off the phone, and every night she would yell back the typical, "In a minute!" After months of this bickering routine, the parents talked with Julie about a regular phone time for school nights. They agreed that Julie could use the phone from 7 to 8 PM. After that her friends would be told that Julie would speak to them the next day. That would free up the phone for other family members. When it got close to 8 PM, Julie's parents would give her notice that the time was approaching. If she went over the limit, they would start to slowly count to 3. If she was not off the phone when they got to 3, she would lose one half-hour of her phone time the next night. They put the new agreement in writing. After all three signed it, they put one copy on the refrigerator and one copy in the parents' possession somewhere in case Julie "forgot" or lost the original. After a few bumpy nights, the plan became part of the routine, and the arguments ceased. Once in a while Julie asked for an exception, and each request was evaluated depending on the circumstances at that time. Her parents let her know how pleasant evenings were in the family since she started sticking to the phone time. Although Julie had been reluctant at first to try this plan, she later admitted it helped her organize her time better, and she enjoyed the improved atmosphere in the family. Her friends originally made fun of her for having restrictions. After they saw the benefits to Julie, they asked their parents for a similar plan.

Teenager: The 1–2–3 approach was helpful to a mother who had daily battles with her fourteen-year-old son. Bobby, a diabetic, needed to have his insulin shot one hour before dinner. He would get deeply involved in playing computer games after school. His mother would start calling upstairs to him to take his shot, but Bobby refused to interrupt his game in the middle, and he would shout back that he would take it "in a minute." This exchange would continue back and forth for over a half hour, with both Bobby and his mother getting more and more angry. Finally, they agreed on a different plan. His mother would give Bobby notice that dinner was in one hour. She would wait five minutes for him to respond on his own. Then she would start counting to 3 over a five-minute period. This gave Bobby a ten-minute range to wrap up his game or put it on hold. If she got to 3, he would lose his computer time for the next afternoon. They put this new plan in writing and both signed it. He felt better that he had some control; his mother was relieved not to have to argue or delay serving dinner because of Bobby's resistance. When the agreement is negotiated together, the child is more willing to accept the responsibility. It also helps to give the child some leeway in responding while still meeting the parent's needs.

The 1–2–3 approach works most of the time and is a helpful tool to have in our repertoire. This technique, like all other tools, will not work all the time. And it will not work at all if it is not consistently followed. But no one approach works all the time. That's why it is important to have a variety of techniques in our parenting tool kit. It's also helpful at times to take a step back and look at the process. If a specific approach is not working after a significant period of time, let yourself be creative and try something new. Trust your intuition. Ask yourself what would work if you were in the child's place.

*When asking our child to do something that she or he may not want to do within our time frame, let the child know you will slowly count to 3. If you get to 3 and the child is not cooperative, there will be a consequence. Express appreciation for the expected behavior, even if you had to count to get it.*

# 11

## Saving Face

PICTURE this scene: We use our 1 – 2 – 3 technique and our child reluctantly gets up off the sofa in the family room and starts to go to bed. As the child passes by, she or he mutters something lovely like "I hate you" or "I'm going upstairs, but I'm going to break all my toys." This utterance comes under the category of "saving face." Because the child lives in a world of Big People telling her or him what to do, she or he often may obey the request but then protest in some fashion.

We need to differentiate between a reply that is a repetitive delaying tactic, a direct disrespectful challenge or a child's way of trying to even the power by implying, "You can make me do it, but I'm going to get in the last word." When it is the latter, as is most often the case, we can ignore the grumbles as long as the child is following through. Backtalk is characterized by insolence, name-calling and rudeness. It is an in-your-face insult that continues the confrontation or challenge. Address backtalk by quietly letting the child know the consequence for such language, then disengaging from the debate. It is all too easy to get distracted by the rude language and forget the original issue. The following vignettes are examples of a child saving face.

**Preschooler:** Many two-year-olds will look the parent directly in the eye and say a loud "no" to a request, even as they are proceeding to do what is wished. Or a child who is reluctant to get into bed at night may acquiesce on time, then ask for a drink of water.

**School-age:** Mom comes home from work and finds Melissa sprawled in front of the television, munching on a bag of potato chips. It is almost time to prepare dinner. Not only is eating in the family room against the rules, she has also left dirty dishes and food out in the kitchen so that Mom can't start to cook. She asks Melissa to clean up the mess. She may even have to use the 1–2–3 method to get Melissa to move. When Melissa does get up, she gives Mom a furious look and starts to handle the dishes roughly. If Mom started to yell at her for the "dirty look" or for potentially breaking something, they will get engaged in an argument. Mom might start attacking Melissa for being so irresponsible Melissa would undoubtedly counterattack, accusing Mom of being too demanding and hard to please. Then Melissa would storm off to her room, leaving Mom to clean up her daughter's mess. Instead, Mom wisely realizes that Melissa's look is a face-saving maneuver. She ignores the protest, the kitchen gets cleaned up and Mom then thanks her daughter for the help. This invites friendly feelings and will encourage Melissa to strive to be more helpful in the future.

**Teenager:** Saving face applies especially to older children. The murderous look and barely audible comment of the adolescent, such as "I hate you," is rarely meant seriously but turns a parents' insides out. For example, Jason, age sixteen, wanted to go over to his friend's house at ten o'clock on a school night. His dad explained that it was too late to be going out. Jason started to argue until both father and son were screaming at each other. Before the argument deteriorated to saying things neither one meant, the father told his son to go to his room. Perhaps realizing that his request was out of line and he was getting out of control, Jason stormed up the stairs to his room. On the way up, he muttered some obscenities, then slammed the door. Dad wanted to scream at Jason, "How dare you talk to me that way. You can't use that language in my house." It took the father tremendous restraint not to follow his son, burst into his room and berate him for his language and abuse of the door. But this is an example of an important time to zip your lips. Dad realized that Jason was trying to save face by acting powerful, but more importantly, he was also complying with the request and the argument was ended. This is one more opportunity to treat our child with respect and dignity, allowing the young person to feel cooperative and powerful at the same time. We then focus on the compliance and appreciate it while disregarding the face-saving gesture.

*After a disciplinary measure or conversation that the child doesn't like, she or he may utter a verbal protest, make a face or mutter one last comment. When the protest is simply a way to get the last word or save face, ignore the behavior, focus on the compliance and when appropriate, offer positive feedback.*

# 12

## Consequences and Choices Instead of Punishment

FOR EVERYTHING we do in life, there are consequences. If we don't pay the electric bill, our lights will be turned off. If we do a job poorly, or don't show up, we may be fired. Parents need to allow children to experience the consequences of their choices in order to learn responsibility.

Consequences are not the same as punishments. The concept of punishing is mean-spirited. It creates hostility and invites retaliation, and it does not teach appropriate behavior.

Consequences can be painful, but also may be positive and pleasant. Research has shown that people learn faster when they are rewarded for their behavior than when the outcome is unpleasant. We learn from both kinds of opportunities.

As parents, we are our child's primary and most influential teachers. It is extremely helpful when teaching acceptable behavior and lifetime values to create meaningful consequences or let the child suffer inevitable consequences. We need to think of painful experiences as opportunities for growth. When we have a pain in our body, we ask ourselves, "What is this telling me? What action do I need to take?" The symptom is a messenger suggesting we need rest, we need to alter the way we are lifting heavy objects or we need to make some other change that will address the problem. Similarly, when we have a frustrating experience or disappointment, rather than berating ourselves we can ask the same questions: "What is this telling me? What can I learn from this?"

Parents often have trouble devising consequences. We do not think we are "creative" enough. However, all of us are perfectly capable of designing actions to teach our lessons. We need to trust our instincts when we get an idea instead of critiquing our own thoughts and saying to ourselves, "No, that won't work." Ideally, a consequence will be directly related to the action being discussed, as in the 1–2–3 chapter: "If you dawdle, there won't be enough time for a story," "If you continue to fight over which program to watch, neither of you will watch TV until after dinner." For an older child, having to write a paragraph about the effects of their misbehavior on others encourages the child to develop empathy and see herself or himself in the context of community.

Sometimes the selection of a consequence cannot be directly tied to a behavior but is instead chosen to have an impact and help a child develop self-control. We use an activity or request that has meaning to the child in order to encourage our child's cooperation with our wishes and family needs. For example, Mindy, age nine, loves to play on the computer. She does not like to do her homework. One day she was particularly out of sorts and was giving her mother a very hard time. Mom said, "Mindy, if you don't stop whining and arguing about doing your schoolwork, you won't be able to use the computer today." Because she wanted to use the computer so much, Mindy finally sat down and finished her work.

Finally, there are situations where we as parents do not need to think up a consequence. We simply remind our child of the natural event that may occur. "If you continue to be so bossy when your friends come over, they may not want to play with you again." "If you don't help me with the chores now, I won't have time to drive you to your friend's house."

One of the hardest moments for a parent is to willingly let your child suffer a consequence, knowing it will be very difficult. Mr. and Mrs. Green knew their daughter, Sharon, age thirty-two, had been battling drug addiction since high school. Because of her problems, Sharon's husband divorced her and got custody of their three children. Sharon had been in a rehabilitation program and supposedly had been clean for a year. When Mr. and Mrs. Green got a call from Sharon saying that she had been arrested for stealing to support her habit, they were devastated. She needed $10,000 for bail or she would have to spend five months in jail. After much anguished consideration, they told her they would not give her the money.

A few months after her release from jail, they went to visit her, not knowing what kind of reception to expect. Sharon greeted them warmly with big hugs. She thanked them for not bailing her out. Through her incarceration, she got treatment, had been free of drugs and was employed in a responsible job. She was feeling strong and confident. It is important to be supportive of our children when they face obstacles or difficulties. But if we continue to make life easy, picking up the pieces of repeated poor choices, we infantilize them and hinder their ability to take responsibility for their own actions.

Sometimes a child says, "I don't care what you do to me" in response to a stated consequence. Do not believe her or him. Too often parents take this statement literally and up the ante, going from grounding for a weekend to staying in one's room for the next year. We need to keep in mind that none of us like to be told what to do or forced to give up a freedom we enjoy. In spite of a child's protests, a consequence will have an impact. The denial is simply your child's way of saving face and not letting you know you are having an effect.

Similarly, parents often think a consequence is not working when a child repeats the same misbehavior. Remember, children learn by repetition so you should continue the consequences. Kids test to see not only where the limits are but whether you are really going to stick to the rules. Be consistent and do not get discouraged. *We are raising responsible children.* It just takes a while. Be patient.

In the spirit of the *zip your lips* approach, here are some further guidelines to formulating consequences:

• Give yourself time to think of a consequence. In the heat of the moment, you will not be doing your best thinking. You can say, "I'm going to think about this. I'll let you know." Your response will have a better chance of yielding an effective lesson, instead of being so punitive that you end up changing or retracting it.

• Consult with your partner whenever possible, especially about a major misbehavior. It is crucial in a two-parent household for both partners to back up the consequence. Don't assign a consequence that you know your partner will not support. It weakens your authority on other occasions as well. It strengthens your position when you can say, "*We* have decided," leaving less opportunity for a child to play one parent against the other.

• Have some consequences established, in writing if possible, for predictable situations.

• Keep it short. Long periods of time lose effectiveness and don't give the child a chance to prove herself or himself. Grounding an older child for one day is more effective than a month sentence. A child will feel the impact of staying home on a weekend with no access to the phone or socializing. When this consequence is extended for a long period or indefinitely, the child becomes more hostile and rebellious. She or he feels there is no hope for leniency so loses any motivation to follow family rules. "I'm already in trouble, what's one more infraction?"

• Time-out or a period of time spent in the child's room after an outburst may be enough of a consequence for certain behaviors. You are trying to teach your child to develop self-control and acceptable ways to express anger. Additional actions to make your point may not be necessary. Name-calling, lecturing and repeating why you are so angry serve no purpose. A time-out can be taken on a chair, stool, stairs or in the child's room, depending on the age and temperament of the child and the severity of the outburst. A guide is to assign one minute of time-out for each year of chronological age. Some children need more time, however, to calm themselves. Other children cannot tolerate isolation for more than a short period. You will sense what your child needs to regroup.

• Offer choices. Choice is power. Power is the privilege of making a choice. State that she or he can do what is needed or choose the consequence. Offer several ways to make amends. When you offer choices, give your child time to decide. Here are two examples:

*a.* I need you to clean up the playroom before dinner. You can either do it now or after you finish your game. If it's not done in time, you will lose your television time after dinner. *It's up to you.*

*b.* After apologizing to your sister, you can write a page on the kind way to treat a younger sister, *or* you can play a game of her choice with her. *You decide.*

When you offer choices and then take a nonchalant attitude ("It's up to you" or "You decide"), the child feels that she or he has more control and as a result will be either compliant or more willing to accept the consequence. You can sometimes ask older children to come up with their own consequence. Often they are harder on themselves than you might be. Also, when you use a phrase like "It's up to you," you put the responsibility for correction and reflection on your son or daughter. You help them to become accountable.

Use positive consequences for the behavior you want to establish. With children who are difficult much of the time, offer something that will be meaningful as a result of less whining and more cooperation. When you use this approach, it is essential to be very specific about both the expectations and the reward. One example is to say to your child, "If for three mornings in a row you get ready for school without an argument, you can pick your favorite meal for dinner." Minimize the reliance on buying things like a new toy or video game. It can get very costly, and most children already have too many toys. Try instead to emphasize spending time together or getting special treatment. Some examples might be sitting in the front seat of the car for a day or week, staying up later on a Friday or Saturday evening, picking the dinner or having a special time alone with Mom or Dad. Children crave time without siblings competing for attention, so a "ladies lunch" or "guy time" is very much desired. Going for a bike ride, playing a game, reading a book together—the activity doesn't have to be costly or extravagant. Make sure that these positive consequences are tailored to meet the child's personality and the family's comfort level.

Behavior modification charts are helpful. Parents should select one to three areas at most to work on at a time.

When we try to change or correct too many habits at once, everyone gets overwhelmed. A chart indicates the exact behavior desired. (Be specific. "Be nice" or "Be less whiny" can be too hard to measure and then lead to arguments.) Indicate when the behavior is to take place. Leave a space to mark if the behavior is accomplished for that time period. Children can receive a check mark, a star sticker or some other indication of completion. A predetermined number of marks results in a positive consequence already selected. The main problem with charts is that parents stop after a few weeks. Once things are going better, they lose interest or think the chart is no longer needed. Accountability maintains the improved behavior.

Why do we need consequences? Why can't children just do the right thing? Are we sending the wrong message for kids to expect a reward every time they do what they are supposed to do or to comply out of fear? Our thoughts are twofold. First, it is human nature to try to get away with something if possible. Many people would speed excessively on the roads if they weren't afraid of a ticket, leading to higher insurance rates. We might pay our bills or taxes late— or not at all—if there were no penalty. We all test limits in some ways, but everyone functions better when we know what our boundaries are. Kids especially respond to clear limitations. When they function within the limits, they feel better about themselves.

Second, we are empowered as parents with the job of shaping our child's behavior so that she or he can function successfully in the adult world. Using positive and negative consequences for desired behaviors helps our child learn self-discipline and the skills to deal with difficult or unpleasant tasks in the future. Our requests and rules serve to make the home operate more smoothly, but they also teach kids the life skills they will need.

*Consequences are a natural part of life experiences. Both pleasant outcomes and negative results offer excellent learning opportunities. Consequences help children develop self-control. They encourage skill development in foresight, planning and decision making.*

# 13

## Keep Your Word

THIS BOOK is about being an effective parent who is loved and respected. One sure way to lose your children's respect is to make promises you do not keep. In a generous mood, you might promise to play a game with your child later, or go to the movies on the weekend. Or, in an angry mood, you declare your child will never be allowed to watch television again. When you do not follow through, your words become meaningless. You lose respect. You lose credibility. You lose ground in your position of authority. Why should your child behave when she or he has learned that your threats are empty? Just as importantly, how can your son or daughter look forward to being with you if you do not keep your promises? Enough said.

 *Keep your word. Say what you mean, mean what you say.*

# 14

## Listen and Learn

THE following poem, by an anonymous writer, incorporates the ideas in this chapter.

### Please Listen

When I ask you to listen to me
and you start giving me advice,
you have not done what I asked.
When I ask you to listen to me
and you begin to tell me why
I shouldn't feel that way,
you are trampling on my feelings.
When I ask you to listen to me
and you feel you have to do something
to solve my problem,
you have failed me,
strange as that may seem.
Listen! All I ask is that you listen.

Don't talk or do—just hear me.
Advice is cheap; 20 cents will get
you both Dear Abby and Billy Graham
in the same newspaper.
And I can do for myself; I am not helpless.
Maybe discouraged and faltering,
but not helpless.
When you do something for me that I can
and need to do for myself,
you contribute to my fear and
inadequacy.
But when you accept as a simple fact
that I feel what I feel,
no matter how irrational,
then I can stop trying to convince
you and get about this business
of understanding what's behind
this irrational feeling.
And when that's clear, the answers are
obvious and I don't need advice.
Irrational feelings make sense when
we understand what's behind them.
Perhaps that's why prayer works, sometimes,
for some people—because God is mute,
and he doesn't give advice or try
to fix things.
God just listens and lets you work
it out for yourself.
So please listen, and just hear me.
And if you want to talk, wait a minute
for your turn—and I will listen to you.

Some children are naturally talkative and tell us a lot about their lives and feelings. But parents of many others complain that when they ask their child, "How was school today?" or "What is going on with your friends?" they get a monosyllabic response and no information. Learning to really listen is a way to share more of your child's internal life and external experiences. *Empathic listening* means giving the child your full attention when she or he starts to talk about some experience. It means commenting only as a way of reflecting back what your child is saying to let her or him know you are paying attention and understanding her or his feelings. It means not interrupting. It means asking a question that requires more than a "yes" or "no" response and does not carry a tone of blame. It involves trying to put yourself in someone else's shoes instead of thinking about your own ideas and feelings.

Finally, listening means not lecturing. Listening is an opportunity to learn, not an invitation to tell your child what you think she or he should have done, didn't do or might experience. Empathic listening is one of the cornerstones of every strong, positive relationship.

As our children got older, I (Renee) learned a lot by driving them and their friends to activities. From my chauffeur's seat I listened to their conversations, which were very interesting. I found that being alone with one child in the car opened the way to some of our best talks. Having one-to-one time in the car with no distractions lends itself to more meaningful conversations. It isn't easy in our busy, everyday lives to make time to just sit and talk together, but it probably is one of the greatest gifts we can give our child, and ourselves.

It seems that fewer and fewer of today's families sit together for a meal. When you have a family dinner, use this time to encourage talking and listening to one another. Try to develop a routine of asking each person at the table something about his or her day. Think of a question that requires more than a one-word answer. Instead of "How was your day?" ask "What did you do today?" or What did you talk about in science class?" Ask questions about social interactions as well, using the opportunity to encourage consideration and empathy for the feelings of others. This sends a child the message that we are not just interested in them as a student or a maker of grades.

If one child tends to be more reticent, stay with that child a while and draw her or him out. There is always a more vocal child who can't wait to tell all, but we want to encourage each person to share, as well as have the experience of being a listener. Some children are very competitive or attention grabbing. As soon as one child says, "I did well on my spelling test," Junior can't wait to interrupt and say, "So did I." We can teach our children good manners and good listening skills (a real plus in future relationships) by practicing as a family. There is a Native American tradition of using a talking stick, which gets passed around the circle during a community meeting. The person holding the talking stick may speak uninterrupted. In families where self-control is lacking or tension is running high, pick a carrot, a pen, a tennis ball—any object easily held in one hand—to represent the talking stick. All others have to wait their turn to speak.

It may be hard to appreciate how helpful it is just to listen when our child is upset. During one therapy session with a mother and young teenage daughter, the girl suggested that she wanted very much to confide in her mother but knew she would only get a lecture about how hard it was when her mother was growing up. Jeannie said she was sick of hearing about her mother's childhood and hearing her mother say that she was overreacting. I asked the mother to promise that we would only listen, that we really wanted to hear from Jeannie and would not comment. Jeannie got a few sentences out with many tears and much emotion. Then her mother interrupted and was also very emotional. In her tirade she said that she knew Sally was not really a friend and that is why you can't trust people and on and on. . . . As I tried to quiet the mother, Jeannie screamed at her, "You see, that's why I can't talk to you," and stormed out of the room. It was a lost opportunity for her mother to learn what was bothering Jeannie and for Jeannie to be able to vent some of her feelings.

There are ample opportunities—after listening thoroughly—to comment or advise if that is appropriate. Sometimes when a person talks out loud, the act of hearing oneself creates the opportunity to sort out feelings and decide on a course of action or inaction. Since we want our child to be strong and independent and able to work out her or his own dilemmas, listening with restraint is a very important and very supportive parenting skill. (It does wonders for the marital relationship as well.)

Just listening, without speaking, is often the "treatment of choice." Another helpful response pattern is the "reflecting back" technique. I often point out to people that in essence we speak in two concurrent languages: one of facts and one of feelings. The words are the surface message, the facts and details of the story. The other message involves the language of feelings. When people are upset, they usually do not want to discuss the details. They are looking for feedback on their emotions. They want to know that their feelings are allowed; they need time and opportunity to express these feelings and to begin to sort them out. When we address only the facts or logical message, we are often surprised by an angry reaction, such as "That's not what I'm talking about" or "You don't understand."

The reflecting back technique is simply repeating almost verbatim what was just described. For example,

*Child:* I had a terrible day in school today.

*Parent:* You really had a terrible day today.

Far from annoying the child, she or he is comforted by the feeling that you are truly listening. You are not going to lecture, correct or change the subject. The child then feels safe to explain more, and we can continue to reflect back the facts of the message to tell the child of our interest and concern.

The second way to reflect back is to comment on the feeling part of the message.

*Child:* I had a terrible day in school today.

*Parent:* You sound really upset (or angry, sad, whatever you sense is the emotion).

Again, by commenting briefly on the feeling part of the message, our child will feel validated and supported. We cannot put words into a child's head by suggesting a feeling. If your suggestion is not on target, she or he will tell you, but the child cannot always identify her or his own feeling without your help. Once, when I was giving a parenting workshop for parents of toddlers, I brought in some books that I found helpful. One mother asked to borrow a book for children titled *Sometimes I'm Jealous.* She had recently had a baby and thought the book would be helpful to her toddler. At the next session she returned the book, saying it did

not help at all. In fact, it made things worse. Now her toddler was running around saying, "I'm jealous." It took some
convincing on my part to explain that she had merely
given her child the word that matched a feeling already
there. He would not have accepted the concept so readily if
it didn't fit.

Sometimes, parents try to be helpful by suggesting to
their child, "That's silly, you don't need to be angry (worried,
scared) about that." When I was young, my grandmother,
who was a very extroverted person, loved me dearly. But she
would get so frustrated with me, telling me how ridiculous
I was for feeling insecure and for being so quiet. Her dis-
dain somehow negated the good feelings I got from her.

We tend to minimize feelings by suggesting that what
happens to children is unimportant, simply because they are
only children. "If you think that's a problem, wait until you
have to pay bills or worry about getting fired." We mean to
be helpful, but the message we send is that we don't take
their feelings seriously and neither should they. Many parents were raised in a family where feelings were not allowed
or discussed. No wonder some grown-ups have a hard time
identifying their own feelings or, if they know what they
feel, don't know an appropriate way to express their emotional life.

Another way of minimizing our child's feelings occurs
when we don't take their account seriously. Many children
try to tell their parents about a teacher who is too critical,
unfair or potentially hurtful to the child's self-esteem. Many
adults were victimized as a child. They recall efforts to tell
their parents about a relative or neighbor who was acting
inappropriately. The parents didn't believe them or didn't

take them seriously enough to question further. Sometimes we don't want to know, consciously or unconsciously, because it would cause problems in the family or create an awkward situation. Because of the potential for lifelong wounds such inaction might cause, we need to create an atmosphere where our children feel free to come to us because we do listen, nonjudgmentally. Then we need to really listen carefully and supportively, especially when the news might be something we don't want to hear.

Of course, we need to know our children well enough to differentiate what may be a true account versus an attempt to place responsibility for their behavior on someone else. When our child has a pattern of turning in homework late or not at all, we will listen to a complaint that "The teacher hates me; that's why I got an F" differently than the same remark coming from a conscientious student who worked hard and wrote a good report. When our child continuously blames others, we can still listen empathically. But we can also gear our questions in a calm, nonblaming way, exploring the details of the situation and asking our child to consider what else she or he might have done to contribute to or alter the event. Here are some examples of empathic listening.

**Preschooler:** Often young children who are used to having the spotlight all to themselves have some unkind words for a new sibling they are supposed to welcome with open arms. You may get upset hearing your three-year-old say, "I hate Baby Joey. Let's give him to the garbage men." Well-meaning Mom or Dad might try to quickly suppress this line of thinking by telling Chris all the wonderful aspects of having a brother. But she is feeling displaced, disgruntled, even jealous. You need to help her label her feelings and really try to imagine what it would be like to suddenly have to share your spotlight. It might be similar to having your husband bring home another woman and say, "This is my new girlfriend. She is going to live with us, and I want you to love her and treat her like one of the family." By trying to sense Chris's feelings, you can give her the tools to express what is going on inside her so she doesn't have to act out those feelings. By accepting her feelings, you will help her to feel understood and therefore comforted, which allows her to also acknowledge her love for the baby. For example,

*Chris:* I hate my baby brother. Let's give him to the garbage men.

*Mom:* You really don't like him. (Reflecting back)

*Chris:* He's always crying.

*Mom:* He does cry a lot.

*Chris:* And then you can't play with me. You have to go to Joey. (Said with a mocking face)

*Mom:* So you really don't like it when I have to take care of Joey because then I'm not with you as much.

*Chris:* That's right.

*Mom:* Maybe we could read some stories together when I finish feeding Joey.

*Chris:* Okay, maybe he would like to hear the one about Frog and Toad.

This is not one of those examples that sounds too good to be true. While the interaction with your child might not go exactly like that, most children have mixed feelings about the new arrival. They are proud, happy and can be loving at times. But they also feel resentful and displaced. By giving verbal expression to the negative feelings, the child can then move on to the positive.

**School-age:** Kids go through many stages where they need to challenge mom and dad. We say they are talking back or being disrespectful. One of the most common phrases is "I hate you," especially when you are disciplining or giving an unfavorable decision.

*Allen:* Can we go to the store and get a computer game?

*Dad:* No, not today.

*Allen:* I hate you! You never do anything for me.

*Dad (Option 1):* That's right (as in Chapter 9).

*Dad (Option 2):* You can't talk to me that way. I never would have said such a thing to my parents, I would have gotten whipped. You are such a spoiled, ungrateful brat. (Breaking all the rules, not allowing Walter's feelings, and also name-calling, lecturing and inviting a hostile debate.)

*Dad (Option 3):* You sound really angry. What's going on? (Allows the feeling, sticks to the issue, invites further communication.) Dad might learn that Allen feels he doesn't see enough of his father, or his best friend just broke a plan to do something and lied about it. Option 3 clearly validates Allen's feeling and encourages further communication.

**Teenager:** Donna, seventeen, has been dating a young man for two years. They have seen each other almost every day and are very close. He doesn't always treat her well, often lying about where he was or why he didn't call. They argue periodically. Recently he told her he ran into a girl he had a crush on when he was in high school. He talked with her a while and then asked her out. He told Donna he just wants to be friends with her now while he dates this other girl. She is devastated.

Over the next weeks, Donna is very sad and cries a lot. When she approaches her friends and parents for comfort, they all try to give her advice, which ranges from dumping him to revenge. While they all care about her and are trying to help, she isn't ready to think of him not being part of her life, nor is she ready to be angry with him. They might even end up getting back together. This would be uncomfortable if her friends told her they never liked him or made other negative comments about him. As Donna cried in the therapist's office, she said, "That's why I needed to come to you. *I just needed someone to listen.*"

Donna is a very bright young woman who knew that this relationship might not be a healthy choice for her. She also knew she was going away to college in a few months, which would have been a natural separation. It wasn't the time to tell her what to do or remind her that her choice of a boyfriend was not optimal. She needed someone to empathize, to try to imagine what she was going through and allow her the space and time to sort it out for herself. In short, she needed someone to simply listen.

*Empathic listening—being attentive, nonjudgmental, trying to understand the other person's feelings—is an important ingredient in a positive relationship.*

# 15

# The Storytelling Technique

ROGER, age nineteen, was the focus of an angry family session. The parents were furious with him because of his irresponsible behavior. He had damaged two family cars due to carelessness, lost a series of jobs and dropped out of the local community college without telling his parents. The tension and arguments at home were affecting the whole family. When I (Renee) talked alone with mom and dad, I learned that dad had several brothers. One was an alcoholic, another had died of a drug overdose. A third, age forty, still lived at home with his parents and was unable to keep a job.

The parents were frightened that Roger was heading in the same direction as dad's brothers. As a result, they were overly harsh in the way they were dealing with their son's behavior. I asked them whether they had faith in Roger. They did not. When they projected ahead five years, they envisioned him in trouble with the law, either homeless or living at home, continuing to drain them financially. I told them about what I call the "storytelling technique." We formulated a picture of Roger in the future that was much more positive. In the next family session, the parents were able to discuss their expectations with Roger in a calm way. Together they worked out a payment plan to reimburse the parents for all the bills they had paid. When they treated Roger as an adult who can take responsibility, he sat up straighter and participated more actively.

All children go through phases where their behavior is difficult and undesirable. They have habits, like thumb-sucking, that seem to be a permanent fixture. At those times, we can get very down on our child—and ourselves, feeling we have somehow failed as parents. If we start to think of our child as permanently stuck in that phase or behavior, we can lock them in to a self-fulfilling prophecy. "They think I'm a loser, so I might as well be one."

A noted psychologist described the pattern of growth as alternating phases of equilibrium and disequilibrium. We all know the unpleasant battles that result when a child is in the throes of the terrible twos or a four-year-old vacillates between clinginess and independence. There are many behaviors during these early years that we want our children to outgrow: waking up during the night, whining, carrying a raggedy blanket, thumb-sucking, tantrums, poor toilet control. Somehow we get through those times because we know a child doesn't go to college in diapers and things do get better. It is wonderfully reassuring to our little one to share this good news.

The storytelling technique promotes a positive outcome. It asks you to consider all that you know about your child and the process we call growing up. For example, you know that children don't go to college wearing diapers. Assess your child's strengths, learning style, flexibility and other qualities that predict success as an adult. Then envision the desired behavior, positive outcome or change, believing in your child. The next step involves sharing that vision with your sons and daughters so they too can see themselves acting in a more mature, positive way. This approach encourages growth and change, as it allows the child to visualize the new behavior.

In business, it is crucial for a company to have a vision of where they want to be in five or ten years. Without a vision, it may flounder or not grow at all, since it has no direction. When you describe the next phase of more mature behavior, your child can work toward that more    positive goal. She or he can put her- or himself into that new picture. Here are some examples of the storytelling technique at work.

**Preschooler:** Mary, age three, just threw herself on the floor kicking and screaming for twenty minutes. Instead of yelling at her, wait until she starts to fizzle out, or maybe just hold her or have her sit in time-out, depending on her age and personality. As she calms down, talk quietly to her, maybe stroking her hair or back as you talk soothingly. "Mary, I know it's so hard to be little, it must feel like you never get your way. One of these days when you are a bit older, you can do more big-girl things, and you won't get so angry if I have to say no to something. I don't know if it will be next week, or tomorrow, or in a while, but I know it will happen."

You are giving Mary a vision of being a little more grownup. She will have more self-control, as well as more freedom. Baby-sitters, older siblings, cousins or friends serve a similar function. Kids observe their teenage baby-sitter and try to emulate their behavior. They model themselves after a favorite cousin or neighbor. We can use the older child's behavior to reassure our child: "Jennifer used to be afraid of the dark like you, but now she sleeps in her own bed without any problems, and you will too."

**School-age:** Every year the teachers would tell Todd's parents how smart he was but that he wasn't working to his potential. He did very well in science because it was his favorite subject, but he put only minimal effort into other areas. Outside of school he had many friends and was very sociable. He would get his buddies to go exploring in the woods or invent something in the basement playroom. Todd's grandmother was a former schoolteacher who believed the parents were too easy on Todd. She felt he was developing poor attitudes and study habits at an early age. He wouldn't get into a good college, and his talent would be wasted. Derek, a neighbor and friend of the family, told the parents not to worry. He noted that Todd was a terrific boy with a natural curiosity to learn. He had been the same way when he was little, and it wasn't until the second half of high school that he became motivated to be a serious student and get good grades. He graduated from MIT and had an excellent job with NASA. The parents reminded themselves that when Todd was interested in a subject, he was thorough and tenacious in his approach to learning. In general, he was a cooperative, lively boy with many interests and good interpersonal skills. They decided to listen to their neighbor's advice and be more positive with Todd. Rather than focusing only on his grades, they found other areas in which to compliment and encourage him. They discussed the importance of grades as a predicator of future class placement, college and career options, but also expressed faith that he would decide what was important to him and would succeed.

Other parents might have listened to grandma and taken a tough approach, emphasizing only good grades. This approach would precipitate battles between Todd and his parents. He would have spent many years hearing that he was not a good student, feeling his parents' disappointment in him. By having faith in him because of his strengths and predicting a positive future, he will be nurtured in his choices and encouraged (not forced) to become a better overall student.

**Teenager:** Dan spent many hours outside of school at home, alone. His parents would encourage him to invite someone over or make a plan with friends. They offered to drive, to sign him up for a class. He did participate in one sport with the school but didn't seem to connect socially with any teammates after the games. He insisted that he liked staying home. Many weekend days and nights he was watching sports or using the computer. In contrast, his sister was a social butterfly. The phone was always ringing for her, and she was rarely home. The parents felt there was something wrong with Dan. He was too shy and socially withdrawn. They took him to a therapist who interviewed Dan and the family. The therapist recommended they leave him alone, since he didn't seem unhappy with his life and was functioning well in school. She predicted that Dan would become more social when he felt ready to do so.

Toward the end of sophomore year, Dan started spending time with a few guys. They would get together and make bets on fantasy teams or rent a movie. In his junior year, his circle of friends continued to increase.

In February, the parents were shocked to learn that Dan had gone to a party. A week later, he was overheard talking to a girl on the phone. Surprising things continued to happen. In April Dan announced that he was going to the prom with a "friend." Two weeks later he announced that the friend was now a girlfriend.

Initially, the parents didn't have a vision that Dan would have a social life, date and marry. They feared he might be socially inept, depressed or in need of help. It was important that the therapist reassured them that Dan was a terrific guy who had his own timetable for social maturity. Although the parents weren't totally sure the therapist was right, they felt comforted enough to back off, worry less and enjoy having Dan around. Now they complain jokingly that they never see him anymore.

What if you really can't see the light at the end of the tunnel, if you don't believe your child will change or outgrow a difficult behavior? It helps to know something about child development, to remember that children definitely go through many phases. The terrible twos are not the only phase of struggle. In their task of becoming independent and differentiating themselves from us, they will try out a variety of behaviors. Appreciating the reality of phases enables us to be accepting and supportive.

It's also helpful to have an older friend or relative whose parenting style you admire. After all, since we have never been parents before, we really can't know what to expect. A friend who has been through it already can remind us that obnoxious, testing, rebellious behavior may be normal at different stages.

We can recall some of our own behaviors and how we changed—for example, fads and fashions that passed out of favor, sayings that were "cool," arguments with our parents or ways we found to avoid doing what they wanted us to do. Most importantly, we can, for the most part, look at our child's whole picture. Consider all the strengths, talents and wonderful qualities of your child. Keep these positive qualities in mind as part of the big picture. Consider the current behavior as a small part of the picture, an area for improvement. Decide what, if anything, you can do to influence growth.

The power of suggestion is well known and not fully appreciated. When we have a thought such as "This is going to be a horrible day," our body feels tense, apprehensive. We begin to worry, to forget things, to drop something, to be irritable. Like the first fall in a chain of dominoes, our anticipated day becomes a reality we set in motion. On the other hand, if we start the day telling ourselves, "I am going to have a really good day today. I'm going to enjoy each part of my day," we set in motion a different chain of events. By telling ourselves our child will outgrow a phase, develop more positive habits and have a wonderful future, we are not being overly optimistic or naive; rather, we are setting up the dynamics for positive interactions and life-encouraging directions with our child.

*When your child is going through a difficult phase or has a habit you want to change, tell the child a story about how much better it will be when she or he is older. Predicting the future where the child will change an undesirable habit or behavior encourages growth and a positive relationship.*

# 16

## Helping Children Talk About Difficult Subjects

RECENTLY, two youngsters hid in the woods of an elementary school after setting off a fake fire alarm. As the building emptied, the boys fired shots into the crowd, killing several students and one teacher. On the news the next day, a psychologist was asked how parents should talk to their children about this traumatic event. She advised a parent to say to her child, "Sweetie, there is nothing to worry about. I would never let that happen to you. We live in a safe neighborhood. None of your friends carry guns." Far from reassuring, this answer is loaded with false promises that no parent can keep.

Life is fraught with tragic events—illness, accidents, deaths, burglaries and sexual abuse, among others. Much as we try to protect our children, and ourselves, from harm, we cannot in honesty guarantee that nothing terrible will ever happen to them or to us.

It is crucial that, rather than dishonest platitudes, we give our children the tools to allay fears and deal with tragedies. The guidelines to do so are as follows:

1. As in other areas of communication, *be brief.* Give your child a simple answer to her or his question. If your child isn't satisfied, she or he will ask for more information or clarification. For example, Tonya's father has ALS (Lou Gehrig's Disease), a progressive and fatal neurological disease. She sees him growing weaker each week. He now needs the help of a walker to move around, and his speech has become somewhat slurred. One day she asks her mom why Daddy is walking funny. Mom explains that his legs aren't working very well, so he needs help to steady him. "Oh," she says, and goes on to another topic. Mom answered just the specific question and did not offer any additional information. If Tonya wasn't satisfied, she would have continued the dialogue. She may be wondering if Daddy will die, but she didn't ask the question. Mom took her cues from Tonya, figuring that Tonya might not be ready to have her fears confirmed. At some point when the father's condition further deteriorates, Mom will have to sit with Tonya and prepare her for her father's death. Chances are, she will ask before that moment arrives. For now, Mom addresses each question briefly as it comes up.

2. *Be honest.* Tonya's mother will answer truthfully if she is asked whether daddy will die. To lie or give false hope erodes the parent's credibility. Especially at difficult moments, children need to feel secure that their

parents are truthful. In the interest of being honest, though, parents sometimes reveal too much. This is often the case with parents who are separated or divorced. Children should not know all the nitty gritty details of who did what. What happened between the parents to lead up to the divorce, the negotiations for settlement or the differences between them are the adults' business, not the children's. If the child asks a question about the divorce, be honest but vague or private. "That's not necessary for you to know. You only need to know we both love you very much and will be involved in your life" or simply, "That's between me and your mother" are appropriate responses. If parents argue a lot, kids may ask, "Are you going to get a divorce?" If you have a basically strong relationship but the air is strained following a disagreement, you can honestly reassure your child that "Mommy and I are angry with one another right now. Everyone has disagreements once in a while. We'll work it out." When a separation or divorce is a strong possibility, be brief and honest, saying, "It might come to that. I don't know yet. We love you very much and will try to make things okay for you." You don't want to promise that a divorce won't happen, then have to recant your statement later. Nor do you want to give your child something to worry about if it may not happen.

3. *Give reassurance that bad things are not likely to happen.* When a child worries about a burglar breaking in, we can't promise that it will never happen. We can say

that it is not likely, based on relevant factors, such as the safety of the neighborhood, the number of people home during the day, the alarm system, dog and so on. Kids often worry about a plane crash if a parent is going to be traveling. We can inform them that the statistics indicate airplane travel is safer than riding in a car. Information, not glib promises, help allay a child's fears.

4. *Help children focus on life at the present moment, letting go of "what if" thoughts.* Some children are so anxious that their parent won't be home when they arrive from school that they can't concentrate all day in class. We lose the pleasure of the present moment when we dwell on what may happen in the future. Answer a child's fear briefly and honestly. Then bring the conversation back to something in the present, focusing on areas they can control. Help Tonya do something for or with Dad now, making the most of the present opportunity.

5. *Prepare children for possible problems* without dwelling on the topic obsessively. We can teach our children to respond to many situations. Young children today are taught not to speak to strangers. We explain that their bodies are private and no one has the right to touch them in certain ways. There are books that help parents talk about good touch and bad touch, giving our children the tools to ward off child abuse. We can teach even toddlers to dial 911 for an emergency. It can be done through play, by pretending Mommy fell and got hurt. One woman went into a diabetic coma,

and her four-year-old daughter saved her life. The child knew to call 911. She told the operator, "My mommy needs help," and the emergency technicians were there in minutes. Children love to pretend, so we can act out several emergency situations in a play setting, at the same time teaching necessary responses. Once we are sure our children know what to do, we don't need to keep reminding them or bringing up the subject. This will only make them more anxious and may lead to obsessive patterns.

Anyone can get through an easy day with no problems. Life is about dealing with the downs as well as the ups. We need to give our children the message that problems and challenges are unavoidable—but solvable. What do we do with problems? We find ways to cope with them. We can reassure our children not that traumatic events won't touch their lives but that they will be equipped to handle them. Keep your tone of voice light and reassuring. Allow time to think before replying to a complicated question. You will find a reasonable answer, just as your children will learn reasonable coping skills for those difficult times.

---

*In talking with our children about difficult subjects, we should keep our answers brief and honest. Prepare them for emergencies without dwelling on problems, so they learn confidence in handling traumatic events.*

# 17

# Got Those Old Guilty-Feeling Blues?

PARENTS speak a lot about feeling guilty. You may be feeling guilty as you read this book, thinking that you have handled so many situations poorly. We feel guilty about yelling too much, not being home enough, losing our temper too quickly or not really listening to our children in our rush to get things done.

By definition, guilt is the fact of committing a breach of conduct. Feeling guilty is the consciousness of or suffering from guilt—that is, wrongdoing. For parents, feeling guilty is less a fact than a subjective thought: "I am a bad parent," "I blew it." We berate ourselves for undesirable behavior, then too often generalize to feelings of inadequacy. Feeling guilty robs us of energy!

I (Renee) started working when our first child was four months old. That was back in 1969. It was rare for a mother to choose to work outside the home. Over the years, when I was talking about something interesting at work, I often received comments from my so-called friends, such as, "That's nice, but I would never leave my children." The dagger of guilt became stuck in my heart and left me with chronic anxiety for about fifteen years.

At some point, when my older two children were in high school, I realized that they were, in fact, turning out okay. I was finally able to stop feeling guilty. I even saw some benefits to the children from my working experience. But I could have made it a lot easier on myself all those years without those guilty-feeling blues.

Feeling guilty makes our body uncomfortable. Metaphorically, it is like taking a mallet and beating up on the insides of our body. We need to learn to transform guilt into more productive energy. How can we do that? Awareness of an undesirable behavior in ourselves (yelling, temper outburst) can be a call to action. Once we take responsibility for our behavior, we develop a plan to change. The focus shifts from what happened in the past to present and future behavior. For example, one of our grown children may call us to talk about a problem. In spite of all we have written and know to be good advice, our first instinct is to start telling them what we think they should do. We have an agreement to try and signal one another, if we are both on the phone, as to when we need to back off and just listen. Sometimes one will say to the other as a gentle reminder, "Zip." We try very hard to encourage and support their growth, not take over the issue for them. Sometimes we slip back into old patterns. Rather than feeling guilty, we make a mental note to watch ourselves next time.

While guilt feelings can be a call to action, they need to also be a plan for acceptance. We can apply the tools in the book to ourselves, such as being positive and complimentary! Focus on all you do to be a parent that is loving, helpful, caretaking. Accept that you come into this job with no training, no manual. We all learn as we go. Every year we learn more about parenting and meeting the needs of our children. Appreciate your efforts to learn and to grow.

This is especially important for single parents. Many people today are raising children alone, either by choice or by circumstance. While a strong marriage is important, there are situations in which separation or divorce is advisable or unavoidable. If you are a single parent, you probably have already spent too much time and energy feeling guilty that your children will somehow be harmed. It is not necessary to carry those feelings with you. Instead, use your thoughtfulness and energy to focus on being an effective parent *now.* Remind yourself of the qualities you have that enhance your child's life.

We want to do a great job. We need to assess how we are doing as parents, but that is difficult. In the business world, an employee receives an evaluation on a regular basis. She or he also gets raises or bonuses that validate worth. Feedback for our parenting efforts is less reliable— even nonexistent. Because children go through alternating phases and tend to be generally self-focused, we can't really say what kind of adult they will turn out to be. Even when our child is eighteen, or twenty-one, she or he is not a finished product. And there are always "well-meaning" voices that seem to take pleasure in critiquing our efforts.

It is important to have Mother's Day and Father's Day, not just for the card and gift industries, but to show appreciation for parents and to teach children to be thoughtful of others. However, children don't truly appreciate us or see us as separate adults until they are well into their own adulthood. Once your children or their friends start having babies, you'll hear them comment on how hard it is. They'll ask, "How did you ever do it?" We may look back sometimes and wonder, too, but the fact is we did do it *to the best of our ability at the time.* We always are less than perfect. We need to keep evaluating our behavior in order to improve it, but we also need to praise and appreciate ourselves. We work very hard. Parenting is the most difficult job!

*Feeling guilty robs you of energy and serves no useful purpose by itself. Use feelings of guilt to make a plan of action and to improve your behavior. You can also learn to be more positive and self-appreciating of the effort you make, every day, twenty-four hours a day, for your children. After all, parenting is the hardest job.*

# 18

# The Team Approach:
# When Parents Disagree

OBVIOUSLY, we don't marry ourselves. We are attracted to someone with similar values and interests, but that person brings her or his own lifetime of experiences, attitudes, coping skills and behaviors to the relationship. It's inevitable that these differences will surface during your parenting journey. They may cause problems from time to time. How can parents deal most effectively when one says black, the other white? There is a role in these conflicts for a "zip your lips" approach.

We are talking in general terms about most relationships. There are exceptions, as when one parent is clearly abusive or out-of-control, and those situations may require professional help. If you are a single parent, you can apply the following concepts in working with your ex-spouse or with others who interact with your children on a regular basis, such as the baby-sitter, grandparents or a significant other.

As a guiding concept, we need to accept differences in our partner's way of handling situations. Moving beyond the issue of right and wrong, we can leave room for two opinions and two styles, without judgment. Children actually benefit from these differences. They know, for example, that Dad is stricter, Mom is more of a pushover. Mom gets angry quickly and gets over it. Dad doesn't lose his cool very often, but when he does, it is a big explosion and he stays angry for a long time. Mom is interested in crafts and reading stories together, Dad likes sports and outdoor activities. Children benefit from learning to read social cues from these two personalities.

In order to thrive, children need to feel secure in the future of their family and home life. When parents disagree in front of children, whether the issues are parental or personal, the kids suffer. Further, when one parent goes against the other in an effort to be "the good parent," no one really benefits. Children feel caught in a tug of loyalty. They may get angry with the "bad" parent and will challenge her or his authority more in the future. That parent in turn will be angry with the "good" one and will unconsciously sabotage the other parent's relationship with the children.

In the Jones family, some mornings Dad would get up and make breakfast for the kids. Kevin would ask for a bagel. Dad would get in the car and drive to a nearby deli, bringing home a fresh bagel for his son. On the mornings when Dad had to leave early for work, Mom was in charge of breakfast. One day Kevin came down to the kitchen. Mom asked him what he wanted, Cheerios or cornflakes. He told her he wanted a bagel. She replied that the choices today were Cheerios or cornflakes. He started to scream at her that he wanted a bagel. When she started to again offer her choices, he yelled at her. She screamed back, telling him to go up to his room. As he stormed up the stairs, he yelled at Mom, "You just don't understand." Dad, who was just going down the stairs to leave for work, went to Kevin's door and told him, "I understand, Kevin."

Dad's comment clearly undermines Mom's approach. It sets up the "good guy, bad guy" dynamic. Mom was furious, first with Kevin and now with Dad. Dad was siding with Kevin against his wife (which Kevin both loves and feels uneasy about). Dad then turns on Mom for handling the situation incorrectly. Another way of undermining a parent's authority is to tell a child who has been disciplined either directly or covertly, "You don't have to listen to your (other parent)." In the process of "rescuing" a child, parental authority and marital peace have been compromised.

An effective response would have been for Mom to tell Kevin, "On my mornings we have cereal; on Dad's beat you get a bagel." Dad needed to just zip his lips, not comment to his son about his wife's behavior. The message is "We have different styles. No one is right or wrong."

---

*Parents inevitably handle things differently at times. By supporting one another and avoiding the "good parent, bad parent" approach, you strengthen the authority of both parents and the security of the family foundation.*

# 19

## When Nothing Works

THIS BOOK contains many helpful tools and techniques for communicating positively with our children and engaging their cooperation. Nothing works all the time with children, but each of these tools will work much of the time for many families. Some parents, however, may feel that nothing works. They believe their children are totally out of control and they have tried every technique. This may signal the need to look at the parental dynamics or to get professional help. Here are two examples of families in need of professional assistance.

The Reed family seemed to be in trouble. The parents slept in separate bedrooms and barely spoke to one another except to make arrangements for the children. They couldn't remember the last time they went out alone together or had a vacation without the children. Mrs. Reed had a very responsible job with a company in another town. She left the house at 6:30 in the morning and rarely returned home before 8:30 in the evening. Mr. Reed worked locally, so he was home to have dinner with the children and help them with their homework and bedtime routines. He felt powerless, because he was always yelling at the kids, but they didn't listen. He also reported tremendous fights between the siblings. It often reached such an emotional pitch that he worried someone would get hurt.

Lewis Reed, age twelve, was very defiant. He was always challenging his parents and the nanny, refusing to do whatever was asked of him. Although he always scored on the 99th percentile in standardized tests, his grades were Cs, Ds and an occasional F. Sally, age nine, had been diagnosed with Attention Deficit Disorder with Hyperactivity (ADHD). She had trouble following through on directions or school assignments. She was very disorganized, talked constantly and interrupted all the time. Mr. Reed tried for months to bring order and calm to his household, without success. Finally, he went to a therapist, who asked to meet with the whole family. The therapist recognized that Sally needed some professional intervention for her ADHD. She also sensed the tremendous tension between the parents, which was affecting each member of the family.

For the Reeds, as well as many other families with serious problems, specific parenting techniques may not be enough to compensate for feelings of tension, hostility and insecurity in the household. Working with a qualified professional can help isolate the issues, develop strategies and give all family members the support and empathy they need to change. Therapy sessions allow communication in an environment where listening skills are developed, respect for each person's ideas is stressed and nonblaming and problem-solving techniques are used. Couples find that working through troublesome issues together brings the experience of intimacy back into their relationship.

Erica, age seven, is another example of a difficult child. Her mother, Irene, brought her for therapy because she would have a temper outburst at home, throwing herself on the floor and screaming for up to an hour. Irene found herself battling constantly with Erica. Much to her surprise, the feedback from Erica's teachers and her friends' parents was that Erica was a well-behaved, delightful girl. I (Dale) met with Erica alone, and I indeed found her to be very likable. However, as soon as her mother came into the room, her personality changed. She was belligerent, whiny and challenging. At the next session I asked to meet alone with the parents. I found the same hostile attitude existed between Irene and her husband. They slept in the same king-size bed but on opposite sides. There had been no intimacy between them for years. They seemed to openly dislike one another.

Erica was not a difficult child. She was reacting to the negativity in the family. She was angry at both parents for the way they were treating one another. She was also frightened, sensing that her family's emotional foundation was not very sturdy and could crumble at any time. When children act up, their behavior can be an unconscious attempt to get the parents to come together, to join forces in an effort to help. It can also be a distraction technique; a child feels unconsciously that there is too much tension between the parents, so she or he will shift the focus to her- or himself. Often parents will seek professional help for their children where they are resistant to counseling for themselves. No one wants to see their child suffer. On the other hand, parents may not feel they have time to help themselves. They may be embarrassed, or they may fear that bringing their problems into the open will only make them worse and result in separation or divorce. In our experience, avoiding problems creates a wider gulf between two people. Learning to communicate feelings and needs in an appropriate way strengthens a relationship.

*Whatever the source of the resistance, a family in which nothing works results in a group of unhappy people who might benefit greatly from therapeutic intervention.*

# 20

## Praise Is Powerful

THE MOST powerful and motivating way to influence children is through praise, acknowledgment and positive reinforcement. Yet if we were to track every interaction during the course of one day with our children, we would find that we mainly speak to them when we want them to do something or when we disapprove of what they have done. It is extremely helpful to comment on the behavior you want to encourage. For example:

> *I like the way you are playing with your brother.*
>
> *Thanks again for helping me with dinner. I really appreciated it.*
>
> *I noticed your room looks very organized. That's great!*
>
> *You got your homework done last night without a fuss. Good for you.*

By calling attention to positive behavior, you encourage more of it. As the saying goes, "You catch more flies with honey than with vinegar." Pavlov, in his scientific experiments with mice, showed they learned to get through a maze faster when they were rewarded with food at the end than when they got an electric shock for making a wrong turn. His studies led to the theory of positive reinforcement. Children innately want to please us and will work for our approval, even though it doesn't always seem that way. We do not have to be phony, nor should we excessively praise every little thing they do. But we do need to verbalize and promote their more mature, responsible and kind behaviors. It is easy to find something positive to say about any sincere effort: a good report, a game, an attempt to be considerate. Make a simple, positive statement, then stop. A "Thanks, but . . . " statement is not positive. "Thanks for helping me bring in the groceries today, but where were you this morning when I needed help?" negates any good feelings of being appreciated. It is important to build positive feedback into every experience.

The way we treat our children is a reflection of the way we treat ourselves. The way we treat ourselves mirrors the way we will treat our children. We can also be role models for our children in our behavior toward our spouse and others. Every time we thank our partner for helping with dinner, doing an errand, changing the diaper or playing with the kids so we could get some work done, we are modeling positive reinforcement. We are also creating a tone of loving good will, which goes a long way to establishing a more harmonious family. Here are two examples.

**Children:** When siblings get into spats and disagreements, we expend a lot of energy yelling at them to stop. They get

attention for fighting. To change the momentum and motivate the kids to work out their differences, call attention to their behavior when it is cooperative and peaceful. Make a point of commenting when there is no fighting. Compliment the times when they are coexisting, or better yet, are playing well together.

"I really like how you two are playing so well together."

"Inez, you are being so patient with your little sister."

"Ira, thank you for entertaining your brother while I was on the phone. I love when you play so well together."

**Adults:** Mr. Kelly wanted to fix a broken door. Mrs. Kelly wanted him to hire a carpenter, since he was not very handy with tools. There were also a lot of constraints on his time due to a demanding job. He was insistent that he would take care of it. As several weeks went by, Mrs. Kelly started to remind him on a regular basis that he said he would fix the door. He kept insisting that he would get to it. Finally he went to a store and ordered the new door. After another two weeks of waiting, the door was in, and Mr. Kelly went to bring it home. He had trouble getting it into his trunk, as he had only a mid-size car. When he finally got home, he had to call a neighbor to help him carry the door inside. As they struggled to install the door, he discovered it was the wrong style. He had to take it back to the store and wait again for the order. Mrs. Kelly in the past would have exploded. She would have called Mr. Kelly all kinds of names and criticized him for being inept and for poor planning. But she had heard of the zip your lips approach, so she decided to keep her silence. Finally the door was installed. Instead of reminding him how long it took him to put in the door and how much better it would have been to call someone when she wanted to get help, she complimented him on the beautiful job. He beamed with pride and felt a wave of affection for his wife.

These kinds of events happen all the time between partners as well as with our children. For example, we are annoyed when something isn't done our way or on our timetable. Someone is late or forgets to do an errand we requested. These events could result in frequent complaints, gradually eroding all good feelings in the relationship. It is crucial to prioritize our comments, saying only those that are most important to express or resolve. My father had a habit of trying to push the bangs off my forehead when I was in high school He would say, "Get that hair off your face. You would look so much prettier." That comment created ambivalence and got in the way of a potentially good relationship. If he had expressed his opinion about my hair one time and then let it go, I would remember more of his positive comments. When we focus on the positive in a relationship, we create harmony and good will.

---

 *Praise is a powerful motivator of behavior. Speak to your child in a positive way many more times throughout the day than with correction, orders or criticism.*

# 21

## Phrases to Eliminate from Your Parenting Vocabulary

*"Did you do it?"*

*"Why did you do it?"*

*"Why didn't you do it?"*

*"When are you going to do it?"*

*"You never . . ."*

*"You always . . ."*

*"If I told you once, I told you a hundred times . . ."*

*"I told you so."*

*"When I was growing up . . ."*

*Any negative comment that is a general statement about the child, not the behavior, as in "You are so lazy, bad, messy, rude, etc."*

*"Shut up."*

*Any kind of name-calling*

*Obscenities*

# 22

# Phrases to Incorporate on a Daily Basis

💜 "I love you."

💜 "You are such a sweetheart."

💜 "Please."

💜 "Thank you."

💜 "I need you to . . ."

💜 "You did a great job on . . ."

💜 "That was a big help, I really appreciate it."

💜 "I love you."

💜 "You look . . ." (Reflect what they might be feeling.) "Do you want to talk about it?"

💜 "I'd like to hear your opinion."

💜 Any positive comment on the child's behavior you wish to encourage.

💜 "I really appreciated it when you . . ."

💜 "Yes."

💜 "No."

💜 "I love you."

# 23

## Conclusion

### Children Learn What They Live

If children live with criticism, they learn to condemn.

If children live with hostility, they learn to fight. . . .

If children live with ridicule, they learn to feel shy. . . .

If children live with shame, they learn to feel guilty. . . .

If children live with tolerance, they learn patience.

If children live with praise, they learn appreciation. . . .

If children live with approval, they learn to like themselves. . . .

If children live with fairness, they learn justice.

If children live with kindness and consideration, they learn respect.

If children live with security, they learn to have faith in themselves and in those about them.

If children live with friendliness, they learn the world is a nice place in which to live.

*—Dorothy Law Nolte*

THERE IS a cartoon of one person seated in an otherwise empty auditorium. The banner at the back of the hall states "Convention for Adult Children of Functional Families." Over the years, we have been struck by the number of adults still carrying the scars of hurtful, unhappy childhoods. The wounds range from the obviously traumatic experience of living with an alcoholic or abusive parent to the more subtle—having a physically or emotionally distant parent; having parents who fought constantly or didn't seem to like each other; hearing angry or critical statements about yourself over a period of time; being labeled a troublemaker, loser or a disappointment; living with the superstition that you shouldn't be happy because it only means something bad will happen; always feeling in competition with another sibling or person and not measuring up.

Adults have other traumatic experiences as a child: the death of a family member, poverty or financial struggle, geographic moves, illness or disability. Children seem to handle these externally imposed circumstances far better than the negative experience of living with a difficult parent. Yet parents don't start out to harm their children. Our intent is to give our children a good home and a loving foundation for their personal development. We plan to fall in love, marry, have a family and live happily ever after.

In this vitally important and extremely difficult job, we are our child's primary and most influential teacher. We want to help our children recognize their potential and feel confident in who they are, what they can do and what they will become. But we come to this job without the benefit of a training program or manual. We start with few guidelines other than our own experience. Many people base their parenting philosophy on the idea of being different from their parents.

*We can learn to become better parents.* Being thoughtful about our behavior, and talking with our partner and respected friends or relatives, can help us reflect and change as we go through problems and stages with each child. We can find role models like an admired teacher or friend whose children are older. Reading magazines and books like *Zip Your Lips* can be helpful. It can also be confusing, so we each need to take the advice that works for us and our family style, disallowing other advice without feeling guilty.

This book is our effort to support parents in the difficult journey of parenting so that all our children can grow up to feel nurtured, strong and confident. We have covered a lot of topics together. These ideas, tools and skills will help us be more effective parents. As we get older, we can get wiser and more mature. No one is ever a finished product; we always keep learning—as do our children. As you begin to incorporate these ideas into your everyday routines, try changing one or two techniques at a time. Trying to remember and change everything at once may feel overwhelming. It is always helpful to take on one or two projects at a time, rather than unrealistically trying to accomplish too much at once. Be patient with yourself and your children as you practice these tools. Give them time to take hold. Do not get discouraged. Give yourself compliments and positive feedback for all the efforts you make to be more effective and nurturing. You are already doing a better job than you think you are. Taking the time to read this book is proof.

When we are brief, consistent and more positive and supportive, we will reap the benefits of a warmer, more loving relationship with our children. By following an instruction as simple as *zip your lips,* we gain the satisfaction of seeing our children develop into responsible, caring and effective adults.

# Index

# About the Authors

**DALE M. JACOBS, M.D.,** is a child psychiatrist in private practice with more than 25 years of experience. In addition, he is a consultant to numerous school districts, providing neuropsychiatric evaluations for Child Study Teams.

**RENEE GORDON JACOBS, M.S.W.,** is a clinical social worker who also has more than 25 years of experience working as a psychotherapist with families in private practice and as a consultant on parent education programs. She pioneered parenting workshops in 1977 and continues these workshops and seminars today.

**ANN HAALAND** creates artwork via illustration, graphic design and photography. Her business, Haaland Creative Services in Dover, New Jersey, provides the artwork for publishing, advertising, promotional, display and packaging materials. She is also co-owner of New Shoes, LLC, creators of "Home Free," the comic strip for people who work from home, which appears in Entrepreneur's *Home Office* magazine.